I0310767

OVERCOMER

Crowned in Freedom

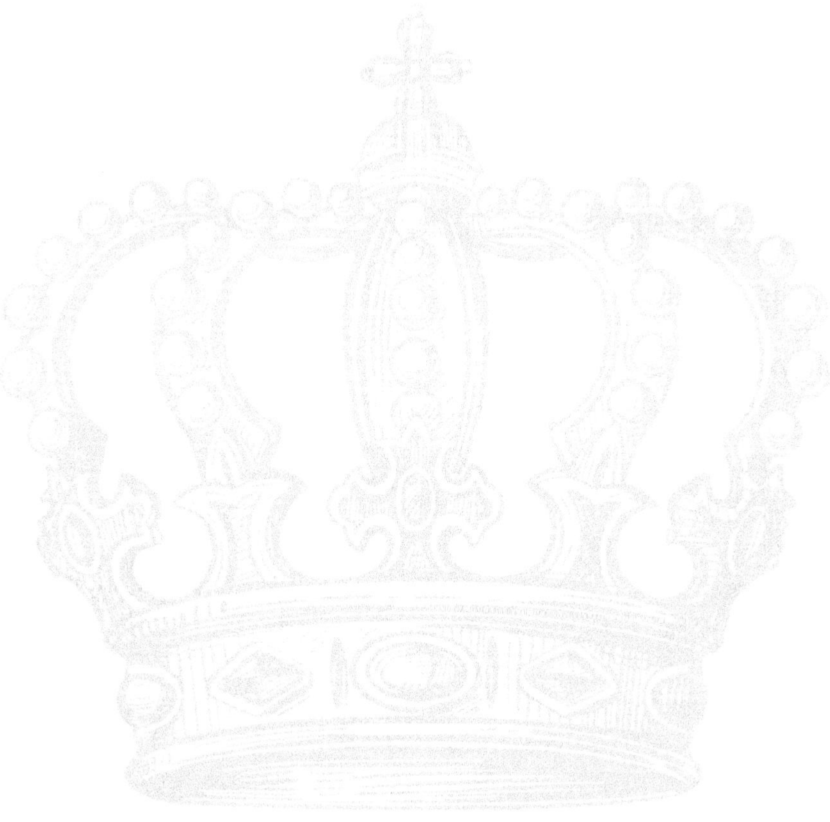

Overcomer - Crowned in Freedom.
Copyright © 2021 by Kylie Smith. All rights reserved.
No part of this book may be used or reproduced without written permission from the author.

ISBN 978-0-6451717-0-9

Book cover - Christina Munns
Book editor - Adam James
Typesetter- Justin Hawkins, Benjamin Mourad
Photographer - Darren Pedley

Disclaimer
This book is sold with the understanding that the author is not held responsible for the results accrued from the advice in this book.

Scripture quotations are from New King James Version (NKJV). Copyright. © New Living Translation (NLT). Copyright. © The Passion Translation (TPT). Copyright. © English Standard Version (ESV). Copyright. © New International Version (NIV). Copyright. © The Message (MSG). Copyright. ©

Author Contact Details:
Kylie Smith
libertylifeconsulting.com.au
kylie.libertylifeconsulting@gmail.com

Acknowledgement

As I sit here and reflect on the completion of my first book, it's almost impossible to describe to you the gratitude I feel in my heart.

First and foremost I would like to thank God. You are my everything and without You I would not have breath in my lungs to be writing this. I am so thankful for Your faithfulness, love and all that encompasses who You are. I am eternally grateful that I do not walk a moment on my own but with You by my side. Thank You for being the lifter of my head. All the glory is Yours!

Secondly, to my beautiful and precious parents; words cannot express the gratitude I have to God for blessing me, by choosing you to be my Mum and Dad. Whenever I post on social media about you two it has the hashtag #blessedwiththebest. That is so very true. Thank you for your constant love, faithfulness and cheering me on, through the seasons and journey of life that has got me to here. I am forever grateful for the gift of you both.

On my journey in life there have been many integral people who have been in my world, that have contributed to the woman writing these words to you today. To the pastors and spiritual mothers and fathers, who have poured into me, believed in me, saw the God potential in my life when I couldn't, thank you! Mark and Darls, thank you for your leadership and for loving people the way you do. Grateful for you both, beyond words.

To my precious friends, the ones that are more like brothers and sisters, I thank God for you, often. You have listened to the desires of my heart come to fruition, have cheered me on and have prayed with me. You have been my 'iron sharpens iron' friends and confidants. You have wiped away my tears and have walked through the frustrations and disappointments during the waiting. Thank you for the encouragement, the challenging and the strength you have brought to my life.

To the beautiful people who have helped in their creativity to bring this book to reality. To Bee, oh my heart! Your encouragement and creative articulation have been a constant during this process, thank you! To Christina for my book cover and your amazing creativity and encouragement, thank you! To Darren for the photos, what a delight you were to work with, thank you! Thank you Benjamin and Justin from Be More Creative for your creative genius, in putting it all together. This book would not be where it is today without each of you. Thank you!

To the beautiful women I've had the honour to pastor, mentor and walk beside on your journey, it has been a highlight in my world to see you shine.

I am blessed to have amazing people in my world and I thank God for you!

Dedication

To the beautiful person reading this book, the one that thinks they are not enough, that feels inadequate, yet to unveil your true worth and value, or the one that measures themselves to the 'perfect' person down the road and the one that has an aching to be more, this book is for you. I hope when you read the pages of this book, your identity starts to have clarity like never before. That you will realise you, yes you, can be all you ever dreamed of. You were born to live a life, a life of abundance and live in total freedom, in every area of your life. You are not to be compared to any other person on this planet because you bring a little piece of the puzzle in this world that no one else can fill. Sit back and let the words on the pages speak to you and minister to your precious heart. You are born to live in abundance, beautiful! xo

I hope you enjoy the moments shared in this book. At the end of each chapter there is the App, which is the application, where I'll ask you questions to provoke action steps. Grab a journal and make notes.

If you see 'Selah' at the end of some text, that means pause and reflect.

Contents

Chapter

	Foreword	vii
	My Story	viii
1	Know yourself	1
2	Disappointment	17
3	Faith	36
4	Intentional living	52
5	Give yourself permission	69
6	Thankful heart	86
7	Forgiveness	103
8	Kingdom	111
9	Freedom	126
10	GO	139

Foreword

James 1.12 (TPT)
'If your faith remains strong, even while surrounded by life's difficulties, you will continue to experience the untold blessings of God! True happiness comes as you pass the test with faith, and receive the victorious crown of life promised to every lover of God!'

Dear friend, we are so excited that you hold this book in your hand. Mark and I know and love Kylie and have witnessed the amount of time, prayer, love and care that has gone into every word, all with the hope of you finding complete healing in Jesus as you read.

Kylie is one of the great pastors in our church. Mark and I have seen her for many years, consistently love people and lead them to the heart of God, which in the end, is where our true identity comes from. This is what OVERCOMER is all about, holding onto HOPE while walking through the storms. Kylie has overcome many unique challenges throughout her life, and her faith has remained strong and her heart has remained steadfast.

I don't know what challenges you are facing or the battles in front of you, that look too big for you, but our great God does. If you live in fear over the miracles you are still waiting for, if you are focused on what you do not have, or what you cannot change in your own strength, then we know these words will remind you that OUR GOD who loves us all with an everlasting love, has already gone before us and made a way. He is the good Father who delights in taking our nothing and turning it into something BEAUTIFUL in its time.

The favour of God upon our lives has little to do with material things. Sometimes He allows a circumstance that looks to us like emptiness or defeat, to invite us into a bigger miracle story.

It is an honour to endorse 'Overcomer', as we are confident it will encourage and challenge you to live a life that will be filled to overflowing, with purpose and true freedom.
With so much love,

Darlene & Mark Zschech xx
Lead Pastors, Hope Unlimited Church

My Story

'You formed my innermost being, shaping my delicate inside and my intricate outside and wove them all together in my mother's womb. I thank You, God, for making me so mysteriously complex! Everything You do is marvellously breathtaking. It simply amazes me to think about it! How thoroughly You know me, Lord! You even formed every bone in my body when You created me in the secret place, carefully, skilfully shaping me from nothing to something. You saw who You created me to be before I became me!'
(Psalm 139.13-16 TPT)

Psalm 139 was my favourite scripture as a girl. I loved the word of God and shared this scripture as an encouragement with many a friend, however, I doubted it was truth for myself.

I knew God loved me and even had a plan for my life, but the part of that scripture that says, 'I'm fearfully and wonderfully 'made', was that really for me, or just for every other person in the universe that has ever been created and was yet to be created? It breaks my heart to even write this now, but I loathed myself. I thought I was the ugliest girl I had ever seen in my entire life. The ugliest person to ever walk the planet.

I was born to beautiful, godly and loving parents who had wanted a baby for years, but they were told they were unable to have children. When Mum and Dad found out the news of their long-awaited baby, they were elated and so grateful to God for their precious gift on the way.

Ten minutes before my arrival into the world, my heart stopped so doctors were standing around ready to do an emergency birth.

'You have a beautiful, baby girl,' they said to Mum, then I was rushed out of the room. The doctor came back and called my Dad in (men were not allowed in the room during delivery in those days) to tell them the news of their 'beautiful baby girl.'

I was born with a very rare condition that remained undiagnosed until some months later. I had an extremely rare congenital condition where my eyes were webbed closed, with cleft lip and palate and my legs webbed up, near my inner, upper thigh. The doctors had never seen anything like this and the mid - 1970s was long before the internet.

The doctors told my parents I would not live the day, then the week and constantly seemed to deliver not much hope for their beautiful, baby girl.

Well, I did live the day, the week and I am currently in my mid-forties at the time of writing this.

Growing up I was always a happy girl, but very broken on the inside due to my scars and unique exterior. I looked different to anyone I had ever seen.

My parents would tell me how beautiful I was and that I could do anything I put my mind to. They did not spoil me, they helped me to be independent and do everything anyone else could do. I so appreciated this, which helped shape me into the woman I am today.

When I was one year old, my Orthopaedic Surgeon went to a world conference in London and met with a team of the best surgeons from around the world. He came back with the diagnosis that I would never walk, as it was agreed by the surgeons that I had 'anaesthetic feet.' My surgeon suggested to my parents, it would be best to amputate so I could get used to artificial limbs at a young age.

My parents said they would need to go home and spend time to pray about if this was the way they would choose to go. I'm ever so grateful God gave me to God-fearing, believing parents. Words cannot express the gratefulness in my heart I feel for that blessing. They prayed, and that week Mum had a dream that I was standing.

They went back and told the surgeon they would not be going ahead with the amputation and would be believing God to do a miracle for their girl. I'm sure you can imagine how that news was received. The doctor was not impressed and said, quite disgusted, that there was nothing else he could do for me.

The following Sunday I stood up, holding onto the coffee table. Before long I was walking around and then nothing could hold me down. I have seen God do miracle after miracle in my life.

I had extensive surgeries to try and fix a lot of the physical challenges I had. I learnt though that I needed surgery to heal my broken heart and I didn't know how that could be done, as there is not open-heart surgery for a broken heart and soul.

I always loved God and had a simple faith. God said it, so that was it! I didn't need convincing.

I had a soft heart towards God and people but had a tough exterior to protect myself, or so I thought. The softie always trying to give off a toughie vibe so I couldn't and wouldn't get hurt. I am, so they tell me, very easy to read, so it didn't work very well.

In my teens, it was my greatest heart's desire to be a wife and a mother, to be married and have four children. I wanted a man to love me the way I saw my Dad love my Mum. I saw my friends have different relationships and I had a deep yearning for that. Someone to love me for me.

— x —

My first serious relationship was with a very loving guy that used to tell me how beautiful I was – he was very sweet. Things did not work out but I'm thankful for the love he did show me while we were together and his friendship afterwards.

I then got to the point that anyone would be better than no-one and I entered a very toxic relationship that was very abusive. After a while, I lost who I was, and I became a shell of the person I used to be.

It happened slowly and without me consciously realising. Others around me could see it, but I could not at the time. I was just thankful that there was someone that finally 'loved' me, no matter what the cost. Interesting what my belief of love at that stage was. I didn't love myself enough to know my value and worth, so how could I expect anyone else to see my worth?

God made a way for me to exit this relationship. There were many years of healing and freedom which proceeded that and lead me to be the woman who's overcome many life challenges and chooses to walk in victory.

I am in no way saying I have made it. What I do know is I'm a woman of worth and value and worthy to be loved, by God, myself and others. I have experienced first-hand the love and freedom and healing, body and soul from my precious Lord and Saviour.

I would not be who I am without Him. My heart explodes at the goodness of God.

I am now a pastor in my local church (Hope Unlimited Church) and a life coach, and have worked with women for over fifteen years in equipping and empowering them to know their true worth and value. I have a heart for women, in particular, who have come out of domestic violence. I have run workshops and support groups and seen many women set free to be the women they were created to be. That is what

I believe I was put on the planet for.

Just like I have a story, you too have a story and a message to share. I remember thinking when I was young, I didn't have a story, I hadn't had this massive conversion from the streets to Christ. I know now that a person's story is a beautiful part of life. It's personal and intricate and just as important as the next person's, no matter how dramatic or simple it may seem to be.

APP

- What is the part of your story you feel is a message you can share with others? Spend some time journaling about it.
- Is there a part of your journey/story you do not like? What is it?
- Read Psalm 139 and allow Holy Spirit to minister to your heart.

Chapter 1
Know yourself

'To thine own self be true.'
(William Shakespeare, Hamlet)

Hindsight is a wonderful thing. I've often thought I would love to have known in my teenage years what I know now in my forties. Unfortunately, life doesn't work like that. Continually growing and changing as we navigate life, offers a rich tapestry of wisdom, grace and refinement. These keys to life are not always available to us when we are young.

When young, we often have to test the boundaries to find out things for ourselves. There is nothing wrong with this process, it's just part of the journey. However, if I see a woman of any age struggling in this part of her journey, my heart is right there with her. I know the growth struggle I've lived it. I've shed tears through it and lay awake at night wrestling with it.

What I can tell you, hand on heart, is that my growth journey has made me into an empowered and freedom-carrying person. With a confident smile, I can tell you I am a woman who is in love with my God and where He has positioned me in this life. Born on purpose for a purpose.

My life purpose has positioned me to work with women in a pastoral and coaching environment. I feel so blessed that this is what I have been called to do. Each day brings a new empowering conversation or an opportunity to have an 'ah ha' moment with women in need.

When I start out the coaching relationship, I give each woman a series of forms to fill out, in order to help them discover who they are. This process is so much more than revealing likes or dislikes. My main goal with this strategy is to assist the particular woman I am working with to define her temperament, or the way she is specifically and beautifully wired. I love seeing the woman in front of me have a revelation of who God designed her to be. To understand how she is uniquely and intricately made, on purpose for a purpose. This is a key step on the path to true freedom.

God has designed us all so uniquely in our mother's womb. We are all given a temperament, very intentionally by God, to fulfil the call He has on our life.

We all have strengths and weaknesses. Weakness can be a beautiful thing, something to embrace. Weakness brings us closer to the heart of God. By understanding our weakness, we can allow God to partner with us to view our weakness or perceived weakness from His perspective. Soaked in love, these areas of weakness may suddenly begin to look different.

When I assessed my form, it revealed that I was stubborn and strong-willed. That was no surprise to me. Growing up in the eighties, being stubborn and strong-willed was looked upon as rebellion. With gentle revelation God showed me that strong-willed and stubborn was the way He designed me on purpose. I cannot tell you how much of a relief I felt. To know that the things I had viewed as weakness, were part of my unique design, lead to such liberation. I didn't have to fight anymore with this side of my temperament or feel ashamed or embarrassed. Over time, I came to realise that my perceived weakness, when directed to be used by a loving Father, actually brought liberation and freedom to others. Amazing!

Now, in saying that, perceived weaknesses do not give us a free pass to behave poorly. It does however, open up the conversation with Father

God for us to begin changing our perspective about those weaknesses.

Through intimacy with the One who designed us, we can begin to bring our whole temperament into the light and gentleness of the Holy Spirt. In this space, no behaviour is right or wrong, it is purely a loving discussion about our unique design. God promises us that He will liberate us from guilt, shame and condemnation. For those in Christ Jesus, we can rest in the knowledge that we enter into a judgement-free discussion. We can be healed from shame and liberated from condemnation. (Romans 8.1)

In order to know who we are, first we need to know who God is.

In Matthew 16, Jesus asked His disciples, *'who do men say that I, the Son of Man, am?'* And then Jesus goes on to ask, *'But who do you say that I am?'* (Matthew 16.13,15 NKJV)

Who do we say God is? Do we see Him as Judge, distant and absent, or protector, Father and friend?

How we see God is very much associated with how we see ourselves. If I see God as a God of infinite love, I in turn know I am loved. If I see Him as Immanuel (Matthew 1.23) God with us, I know I am never alone.

One thing I've noticed, when working with women, is that their relationship with Father God can often reflect the relationship they have with their earthly fathers.

Growing up, I thought my parents were the strictest parents in the world. Coupled with my stubborn and strong-willed temperament many a heated discussion was had over the dinner table as you can imagine.

Now, as an adult and a mother, I can see the example of a godly family.

My Mum and Dad honoured one another, as I believe God designs a godly marriage to be. They loved their children, believed the best for them and brought them up in the ways of God, and loving the house of God. I am forever grateful for the boundaries they set with me and for raising me to have a godly purpose for my life.

Often, I have shared that I have the intimacy with my heavenly Father because my earthly father first displayed that to me. He is a big, strong, manly man, but get him talking about the things of God and the saving grace of God and he will share his emotions and shed tears with free abandon. I've seen my Dad set up disciplines to put God first in his life, in his devotion and his family. My Dad shares his faith unashamedly and has a real evangelist gifting. To me Father God has always been present, loving, kind, wants the best for me and believes in me because that's how I felt my Dad was with me.

This is not the case for everyone. I've come to realise that my experience with an earthly father is not the experience some women have lived through. My heart aches as I listen to women who have only experienced emotional rejection, unkind words or abandonment.

I am speaking to you dear one, the one reading this book. If your earthly father was absent from your life, or maybe he lived with you, but was emotionally distant, it would be easy to understand that your experience of Father God would follow this same pattern. This pattern can often influence the way you view yourself.

For example, if I see God as distant and absent, I in turn will believe I am not worthy of love or that I am not enough. These two beliefs, who God is and who I am, are the most common convictions that I counsel women on.

There are so many tests out there to get to know ourselves and our personality type. I would encourage you, if you haven't done so already, to do some online tests. They can offer the beginning framework, that pieces together who you are.

It really does help see the 'why' behind your common reactions and it helps you to understand other people and why they react the way they do.

Having an understanding about the 'why' behind common behaviours and reactions, allows us the freedom to view these through a lens of non-judgement. A behaviour, once we are aware of it, is something to be observed without bias and offered grace and compassion. We all have pain from our past, that is linked to the way we may speak, act or even act out for attention. These trigger points are exceptionally valuable to understand in ourselves and in those we have relationship with.

For example, after being with people all day, I understand I need time out, to just be, to rest and allow Father God to fill me up again so I can continue to give. This is a part of my temperament and the way I was designed. Other temperaments get their energy from being with other people, so having time alone would be the last thing they would want to do to recharge. Without understanding the why behind my need for time to myself, some may feel like it is rejection when I need to set this boundary. Now that I understand, that having time to myself is part of the way I was created, I can set this boundary, knowing it is the most loving thing I can do for myself and others.

> When I know and understand the way I function, I then in turn, set myself and those around me up for a win.

Around a decade ago, I engaged with a life coach. I've been a person who has seen the need for continual growth and accountability. Engaging in life coaching helped me begin that journey of growing into the best version of myself.

Early on, my life coach asked me about my values. As reflective and self-aware as I am, I had not taken the time to articulate my values. My homework was to write down fifty of my values, then get it down to twenty, then ten, until I was left with my five top values.

After discussing my top five, my coach explained that every major decision I make, a new job, moving, life partner etcetera, should be filtered through my top five values.

My top five values are:

- Faith
- Freedom
- Justice
- Authenticity
- Integrity

When I look at my profile and my temperament, these completely fit the way I was created.

I know that if I see injustice, if I see people mistreated or not shown dignity or fairly treated, it triggers something in me. If I see people behaving in a certain way publicly and behaving the opposite way in private, it presses a button in me.

On studying these things further and training others to understand their triggers, it has been incredibly empowering to know there are tools that we all can use to help us respond with love to these triggers.

This does not mean the process of responding rather than reacting to triggers is easy. It first takes the courage to identify what your triggers are and then patience to practice, responding differently, when you become triggered. The main thing is to be kind to yourself as you practice. It can take years of practice to find the desired response to your particular triggers. I can assure you that the journey is worth it. To understand yourself, brings a deep sense of peace and comfort. In knowing that you are not at the mercy of your triggers, can begin to bring a sense of order and calm resolve when dealing with difficult circumstances. It also really helps those around you, when you have a deeper understanding of yourself.

It is so liberating to know who you are and to be free to be that person. I understand this is a journey, and one we continue to take until the day we take our last breath.

I've found the older I get, the more comfortable I feel in being me. I remember a time in my thirties, when this feeling of comfort in who I was just arrived one day. I didn't have to force it or strive for it. The arrival of this feeling strengthened my sense of identity. I do know I made some intentional choices to get me to that place. I continued to practice the choices and sometimes had to choose them through gritted teeth, but, it is possible to set ourselves up for a win in this area.

These intentional choices I made were as follows:

1. I planted myself in a local church. I will go into the importance of this in more detail a bit later.

2. I engaged in counselling. There is nothing wrong with getting help. If I had a broken leg, I would go to the hospital to get it checked out, plastered and leave with a cast on my leg. I know some people think it is embarrassing or shameful to seek help from a counsellor or from a psychologist. But let me encourage you; if something in your life feels like it could use some tender care, sometimes we need professional help in that area. Emotions need healing just as much as our physical body at times, needs healing.

3. I engaged in prayer counselling. There are many of these options around. Years ago, I did VMTC, (Victorious Ministries Through Christ) Ephesus, Healing Rooms and of more recent times, Sozo. Now, I have two beautiful ladies, in our church, who I go and see twice a year, or as needed, to have prayer. I have seen much fruit and freedom come from engaging in prayer ministry. Please be sure to source reputable people.

Regarding points two and three above, my firm belief is that God is my Healer. Full stop. Exclamation mark! I believe He heals in many ways and He has also given people in the medical field, gifts, wisdom and talents to be able to do what they do.

When I was younger, I was booked in to have surgery. A woman in our church questioned why I was choosing to have surgery. 'You should believe God will heal you', she exclaimed. I remember feeling confused about this and went home questioning my faith.

One of the many gifts God has given us, is wisdom. My first point of call is always God. I do not think He gets upset by us using modern and natural medicine. To date, I've had thirty-three surgeries. Each one has helped me and I know God lovingly placed those medical and surgical people into my life so that I could keep on fulfilling my purpose.

4. I invested in relationships with people whom I could be real with and I could call if I was having a bad day. Over the years these people have kindly kept me accountable and at times, have been my rock-solid, cheer leaders. I call them my 'iron sharpens iron' friends. We challenge and encourage one another, they are safe and love beyond themselves. They are priceless.

As iron sharpens iron, so a friend sharpens a friend. (Proverbs 27.17 NLT)

> Who I am is not based on what I feel,
> it's based on who He says I am.

I want to ask you, who are you? Do you know who you truly are? In the depth of your soul, the way God has wired you. I encourage you to go on an adventure of finding out who you truly are. You may learn things about yourself and have the 'ah ha' moment of 'that's why I do that' or 'that's why I get passionate about this.'

Who does God say you are? There are so many scriptures on what He says about you.

After meeting and hearing a woman's story, there's a coaching exercise I like to do. I use their temperament profile, to ask two important questions: What narrative has she been telling herself? And what personal truth is she believing?

Let me explain why I ask these questions. We live out of what we believe. Things that happen to us, go through the filter of our temperament and what we truly believe, at our core. I'll give you an example. Growing up, my parents would say to me 'you are beautiful Kylie.' My personal truth was 'I am the ugliest person in the world.' For many years I lived under this personal truth, which was in fact a lie. People could say things until they were blue in the face, but my mind would filter the lovely kind words said and interpret what I believed. Once we have discovered the person's personal truth, or in most cases, a lie they have been believing, my heart bursts with excitement, as we both allow Father God's truth to be spoken over the lie. Father God's perspective over some of the lies or the 'old tapes' we play on repeat in our heads, is more beautiful, kind and loving, than we could ever imagine. Truth is one of God's continued pleasures He keeps offering us. 'Come discover what I believe about you,' He whispers, 'Let Me tell you who I know you are my very much-loved daughter.'

John 8.32 (NKJV) says, *'And you shall know the truth, and the truth shall make you free.'*

Once we discover the truth, the heavenly truth about the beautiful woman sitting in front of me, I'd ask her to write that truth in lipstick on her mirror, when she got home.

The most common personal truth I have come across, is 'I am not enough.' The heavenly truth is 'I am enough.' This is the truth that I ask them to write on their mirror. Every time they go into the bathroom and see the truth written on the mirror, they are to speak it out loud, whilst looking at themselves in the eyes. If they think about it, they are to say it. I have seen breakthrough come into many lives, using this simple, yet effective tool. It's so important what we believe. It shapes the very essence of who we are.

We will talk about mindsets a little further in the book, but research has proven we can change our mindsets. Altering our self-talk and speaking life over ourselves, is a wonderful place to begin and a very powerful tool to have in your tool belt.

LABELS

In order to find out who we are, often we have to strip things back and remove some labels first. Labels may have been put on us by others or we may have put them on ourselves. When you are in an environment, of hearing a message, and it is reinforced, this can become part of who you are and therefore affect the way you live your life.

As I shared earlier, I believed that I was the ugliest person ever to walk the earth. Kids at school reinforced this, people's constant stares confirmed this in my young mind and in turn, I lived out of a sense of being ugly. I felt it, I believed it to be truth and therefore I lived it.

The things I've heard people share, the words that have been spoken over them, have had an enormous effect on their lives. Words spoken and continually reinforced can be life-changing for a person, either negatively or positively. I have heard it said, it takes one hundred positive things to counteract one negative comment. Working with people over the years, I have seen this to be true.

There is another exercise I do in coaching that I have found to work well. The humble sticky note.

I use a sticky note and get her to write the words that have been personal truths for that person. For example, I am not enough, I'm ugly, I'm fat, I'm dumb, or whatever personal truth applies to them. I then get the person to stick the sticky notes all over herself.

Here comes the power moment. I then gently ask that beautiful woman to walk around the room and say the heavenly truth to counteract the newly discovered lie, that has been written on the sticky note. As she walks with purpose and declares that REAL truth, healing tears often flow, as she takes with an empowered hand those pesky, lying words off.

> Truly knowing who you are can bring liberty to your world and the way you live.

I wonder what labels have stuck on you? Maybe they've been put there by others and maybe there's some, you've put on yourself. They may be from a parent or loved one, a teacher, a pastor or a significant other. If you have some of those pesky labels and you are ready to discover who God says you are, would you do the exercise above?

Take a moment, to write down the personal truths you are walking around with and put them on a sticky note. Stick them to your body

– this takes bravery. Close your eyes, breathe deeply and slowly. If it helps, listen to worship music. With an open heart offer those labels up to the One who designed you and created you on purpose. Ask God and really listen to your heart, about those labels. Do you want to carry those labels into the next chapter of your life? Are these labels good for you and your heart?

It might be helpful to be aware of what triggers you. Are there times where you lose it so-to-speak? That is called a trigger and it presses on something deeper that you believe about yourself.

A few years ago, I was on a cruise, with four of my friends, to celebrate my fortieth birthday. One evening we were sitting in the lounge, listening to a guy sing and play guitar. It was very relaxing and an enjoyable night. One of my friends went up to the guy and asked him to serenade me with the song 'You're beautiful' by James Blunt. I could see she was up to something. When she came back the girls moved the chairs, to surround me, so I could not get out. They knew me well.

What happened next shocked me and my friend too, I'm sure. The guy came up and did just what my friend asked of him. I was embarrassed and tried to get out of this situation. As the girls moved the chairs closer, I felt trapped. I pinched my friend's leg so hard I left a big mark on her! I did get out of there and went to another area of the ship. I was angry and more emotional than I usually would be. After reflection, I realised, that incident triggered me from primary school days. I was shocked because this was something I thought I had dealt with, years earlier. There are always layers.

In primary school, on the way home from school, there were five boys who would surround me, kick and punch me. Now on the cruise, I was totally safe, I was not being abused in any way, however my brain, went back into a moment thirty years earlier, to a time I wasn't safe and was surrounded and felt fearful. Now this painful memory was not an excuse to ever abuse someone else in return, as I had done, pinching my friend's leg. I was triggered. My number one need, revealed in my temperament, is security. I did not feel secure at that point on the ship.

My friends act, whilst pure in its intention, resulted in an unpredictable outburst of behaviour. This was a strong wake up call. I needed to develop a tool to practice, should I feel my safety was under threat.

My trigger in the situation was fear of attack, the personal truth was 'I am not safe.' I knew I needed to take this trigger and my label to God and ask for His perspective. This is exactly what I did. The revelation that came from God was this: If I was ever in a situation, where I was triggered by being boxed in or surrounded against my will, by people or objects, I would say to myself, 'Kylie, you are safe, you are secure.' This was the heavenly truth and the new mindset I had to practice in order to respond to the trigger of under threat or fear of attack.

It is good to be aware of our triggers (hopefully before we're triggered) to set ourselves up for a win.

If you tend to react to things people do or say, I'd love to encourage you to ask Holy Spirit what is triggering you.

In moments of being triggered you have a choice. Are you going to react and get into agreement with that rejection or get into agreement with the truth that is you are totally accepted, significant and secure?

Can you think of someone in your world who just looking at them triggers something in you?

There are many facets of God. As we are created in His image, I believe each person reflects different facets and the nature of God.

Years ago, I was having a personality clash with someone in my world. One day I had a revelation. We both reflected different parts of the image of God. I thought I was the right one (I have since discovered part of my temperament thinks that) and this other person was wrong and wasn't displaying godly character or behaviour.

That day was a defining moment, standing in church, in another state, when God revealed this to me. It changed my relationship with this person forever. Yes, Jesus was loving, kind and compassionate. He was also strong, black and white and firm in His beliefs. Every person is made in His image; therefore, every person reveals different facets of God. It's up to us to choose to look for the multi-facets of God in ourselves and in others.

Let's look at some of the multifaced aspects and names of God.

I AM, Yahweh, (self-existent One) Alpha, (beginning) Omega, (end) Yahweh Rapha, (Healer) Yahweh Maccaddeshcem, (sanctifier) Yahweh Rohi, (shepherd) Yahweh Shammah, (present) Jehovah Jireh, (provider) Yahweh Nissi, (The Lord our banner) Yahweh Shalom, (peace) Yahweh Sabaoth, (Lord of Hosts) Yahweh Ghmolah, (God of Recompense) Elohim, (God is creator, powerful and mighty) El-Elyon, (Most High God) El-Gibhor, (Mighty God) El-Olam, (Everlasting God) El-Roi, (Strong one who sees) Abba, (Daddy) Comforter, Counsellor, Deliverer, Way, Truth, Life, Everlasting Father, Faithful, Lamb of God, Lion of the tribe of Judah, Love, Messiah, Physician, Prince of Peace, Redeemer, Rock, Saviour, Servant, Shepherd, Strong Tower, Teacher, Vine and Immanuel. (God with us)

So, when we look at who God is, it is then we can see ourselves. Let me put it like this ...

God	Me
Jehovah Jireh (Provider)	Provided for
Jehovah Rapha (Healer)	Healed
Saviour	Redeemed
Strong Tower	Safe and Secure
Prince of Peace	Peaceful, calm
Love	Beloved
Vine	Connected
Immanuel (God with us)	Never alone

I find this eye opening. Wow! When I see who God is, truly is, the very essence of who He is, I in turn can see who I am. This is who I truly am, the truth of who I am. I am not the labels that have been placed on me, I am created in the image of the Most High God, I am provided for, healed, redeemed, righteous, safe and secure, full of peace, beloved, connected and never alone!

I'm hoping after you have read this, you will embark on an adventure of discovering the real you. The you God created you to be. Ask Him to show you how He sees you.

APP

- Write down your top 5 values. Begin at 50, then get down to 20, then your top 5.
- If you haven't done so already, have a go at some personality tests.
- List some characteristics of who God is and who you are.

God	Me

Chapter 2

Disappointment

'Hope deferred makes the heart sick, but a dream fulfilled is a tree of life.'
(Proverbs 13.12 NLT)

I'm sure every person walking the planet has encountered disappointment, at some stage in their life. Disappointment is defined in the Oxford Dictionary as; *'Sadness or displeasure caused by the non-fulfilment of one's hopes or expectation's.'*

Where I am today, in my mid-forties, is not where I'd imagined. Some areas of my life have exceeded my dreams and expectations, other areas are a long way off the desires I have had for myself.

Although I started working in my early teens, a career was not my main ambition. I longed and dreamed about getting married and having four children. Being a wife and a mother was my greatest heart's desire for as long as I can remember. Four boys, with one set of twins. I had it all worked out, from my wedding to family life.

I would daydream about being in church, standing next to my godly husband, our hands raised in worship, with our four boys loving God with their whole hearts. But things don't always work out the way we plan.

Twenty years single, again, I have felt the waves buffet me, as I wrestle with disappointment. I have felt the pain of a sick heart as I have lived with 'hope deferred.'

The second part of the scripture in Proverbs, tells us '*A dream fulfilled is a tree of life.*' (Proverbs 13.12 NLT)

Acknowledging disappointment is the first step in moving forward and living from a place where your 'tree of life', can be fulfilled and bear fruit. But acknowledging disappointment is not always easy. Many times, sometimes on a daily basis, I have had to choose to lay down my disappointments and trust God with them, whatever that may look like.

This can be a challenging exercise. However, I can assure you, going to Father God and vulnerably giving Him your disappointment gives you the freedom to remain sweet in the midst of waiting for your dream to be fulfilled. This trust comes from intimacy with our Father who ultimately has the best plans for us. He longs to see us living from a place of hope and promise.

In Jeremiah 29.11-13 (NIV) we can hold fast to this promise; '*For I know the plans I have for you declares the Lord. Plans to prosper you and not to harm you, plans to give you hope and a future.*'

Many of the women I see are getting to the end of their child-rearing years. They long for the happy family they dreamed about as a younger person and are fearful that they won't find a husband in time to create a family or bear children. Some of these women say they do not feel complete being a single woman in this world.

If you have had this feeling, first and foremost, I want to remind you ... YOU ARE A COMPLETE PERSON and no person is designed to complete you.

A mate is to compliment you. You are already complete and created in a design most holy and beautiful.

Colossians 2.9-10 (NLT) says, '*For in Christ lives all the fullness of God in a human body. So, you also are complete through your union with Christ who is the head over every ruler and authority.'*

Based on that wonderful scripture, we can know we are complete in Christ Jesus. There is nothing more we need to do, there is no husband or person we need to find to complete us.

> We are enough and we are complete!

I don't know how many beautiful people I've spoken to, who in their desperation and discontentment, have settled to be with someone who was not their equal and have lived to regret the decision of settling.

Another disappointment I had, occurred around fifteen years ago, in the area of healing.

A friend and I went to see an international minister in Sydney who was renowned for his gift of healing. We arrived early and there was a team of his people, doing individual videos of the ones who had come to receive a healing miracle. There would have been about one hundred people there early, to go through the process, me included.

Hours passed and my friend and I were seated in the reserved seating, where the minister would come out and pray for us.

In the hours of waiting, I was dreaming that after my miraculous healing, I would call into my parent's house and surprise them on the way home. Arriving at midnight, in itself, would have been a massive surprise, but I knew they would have been beyond happy about this wake-up visit. Of course, they longed to see their daughter healed and whole and I don't think they would have minded what time I dropped in, to wake them up and share that great news. My next stop would be to the beach, to walk along the sand.

The time had come, and the place was pumping. It was a sports arena and there would have been thousands of people there. Adding to the excitement, God's presence was so evident, and faith and anticipation were rising.

The minister was out speaking on a microphone, with his video team following. Every detail of his interactions, with those being healed were being played on a big screen.

My friend and I were so excited, and I cannot explain the hopeful expectation I felt. My heart was exploding with faith and basking in the deep presence of the Holy Spirit.

Growing up, I was out on many altar calls for healing. I had stood in many healing services and believed that I would be healed. For years and years, I had walked away from those altar calls, with small glimpses of healing. Even still, I never lost hope. I continue to believe for a creative miracle in my body and that I will walk in the fullness of my healing.

Tonight was different from those altar calls, the presence of God was palpable. The international minister carried such a powerful gift of healing. I was thinking, 'this is my time!'

The minister was praying for lots of people. Many people had creative, physical miracles. Others were set free from addiction and oppression. It was wonderful to be a witness to such miraculous outcomes for people and my heart was full of gratitude to God.

About forty-five minutes later, he was right in front of us. In my heart I readied myself. I thought 'right it's my time now.'

After the minister finished praying, for the person in front of me, he stopped. Suddenly, he turned around and went to a totally different area. He walked in the complete opposite direction and away from where the people who had previously arrived early, had been waiting. Just when he was right in front of me, I was ready, this was my time and just like that he walked away.

Inside I was screaming, like Rose on Titanic, screaming for Jack. 'No, come back!' It was a moment, if I'm honest, of intense grief and disappointment.

I would be lying if I said I didn't shed a tear on the way home. I grieved for myself, but also for the lost moment of when I would be able to wake my parents and we could all celebrate the miracle I was expecting God to perform that night. Even though my parents didn't even know I was at the meeting, I grieved the loss of not being able to surprise them. After all, my parents and I had been believing God would heal me for many years.

After the intense feelings of loss had passed, I remembered that my healing was in God's hands. Even though that night was not my night for complete healing, my heart was truly happy to see many, many people set free.

These examples do not change the truth that God is good, always, always good and that He is the Healer. All things are in His perfect timing.

I invite you to consider this scripture from Romans 8.28.

'And we know that all things work together for good to those who love God, to those who are the called according to His purpose.' (NKJV)

As we discuss waiting in the next few pages, I invite you to meditate upon the truth that 'all things work together for good.' There is nothing lost in the waiting and no decision we make during the waiting, even if it may be perceived as a mistake or the wrong decision, that can result in God's goodness being removed from us.

In the Waiting

It's very important, how we deal with disappointments and position ourselves during the waiting as many promises take time to come to pass.

Let's look at Joseph from the Bible. When he was seventeen years old he had many dreams, but out of immaturity he shared his dreams with his jealous brothers. When Joseph was Pharaoh's right-hand man he was thirty years old. Thirteen years of a journey, where God was preparing Joseph to be the man he was created to be, to rule a nation.

There were many disappointments and betrayals for young Joseph. He was sold by his own brothers into a life of slavery. I think that would have to be up there with one of the greatest disappointments a person could live through. Your own siblings wanting you dead and out of the family, forever. This act would have caused Joseph indescribable pain and loss.

> There is always a season of waiting between the promise and seeing that promise come to pass. What we do in the waiting season is crucial.

In life, we always have choices and our choices have consequences. Some good, some not so good. However, as the scripture in Romans 8 (NKJV) tells us, *'All things work together for good.'* God is creative in this area. Even not so good choices can be worked together for His glory.

Now in saying this, I understand that some things we go through, are not from choices we've made. Like Joseph, he didn't choose for his brothers to get angry with him, to want to kill him and ultimately sell him into slavery. I'm sure there were times he was wondering, if his dream was even real, let alone if he would see it unfold in his lifetime and become a reality.

Joseph could have been negative and despised the waiting seasons. Most would say that a negative reaction to 'the waiting', would have been understandable. We've all been there, even with a small wait, such as sitting in a doctor's surgery or waiting in an airport to board a plane. We've all felt the foot start to tap and the eyes begin to roll, and the deep sigh escape our lips as we have WAITED.

What we can learn from Joseph, was how he actively chose to position himself in each season he was in, on the way to his promise. Whether he was in the pit, in the prison, or on the way to the palace, Joseph was a man of integrity, a man who stayed focused on the promise and the promise-giver, despite what was happening around him. We can do this too.

Another thing we can learn from Joseph, is even though we may make a choice to act on our own to hurry along God's timing, He is always gracious to use whatever circumstance we may find ourselves in, for His glory. Even in Potiphar's house, Joseph's leadership qualities were developed. In prison, he had time to practice interpreting dreams and serving others. All of these gifts were developed and grown during 'the waiting' and ultimately made Joseph the kind, wise and compassionate ruler of a nation he was destined to be.

I'm sure we all have been in a waiting season, on the way to our promise. The waiting season can be short or can go on for years and be pitted with continual disappointments.

For myself, finding a husband was such a yearning in my soul. I was so desperate to be married, or probably more to be loved by a man. In my impatience with God's timing I settled for the first man that came along, instead of waiting for God's mate He had planned for me.

I made a conscious decision to move forward with a relationship, knowing it wasn't right. I made this decision, in fear of my heart's desire not coming to pass. I did get my dream, to be a wife. I did get what I thought would be my greatest heart's desire.

This choice, due to many circumstances beyond my control, lead me to be divorced and a single mother a short time later. Heart break would be an understatement, to say how I felt after my marriage fell apart.

We all know what happens when we take matters into our own hands. Look what happened with Abraham and Sarah. They were given a promise of a son and it didn't happen when they thought it would, in their desired timing. God gave them a promise, that seemed impossible.

Promises in the face of impossibilities is where God does His finest work. He is always finding ways to delight us.

When the promise was delayed, Abraham and Sarah took matters into their own hands.

They had a great idea to help God with the promise. I don't know about you, but I too have thought I would help God to fulfil His promises to me. To 'help' Him bring them into existence, a little faster.

I can tell you, it hasn't had great results. In fact, 'helping God out' to do things, within my timelines and expectations, has not been amongst my wisest choices. And as we know from the Bible, there were consequences to the choices made by Abraham and Sarah.

Imagine how Ishmael felt, growing up, knowing he wasn't the 'promised son.' What about Hagar the mother of Ishmael. I would definitely have felt used and discarded in this scenario.

God was merciful in this as He always is. Sarah gave birth to Isaac. The promise. God didn't need assistance in bringing the promise into reality.

> God doesn't need help bringing
> His promises into existence.

There is so much we can pick apart from this story. The clear message is that God doesn't need help with delivering His promise. He wants us to position ourselves, to do our part and let Him do the impossible. When we partner together in alignment with a loving God, that's when miracles happen. After all, as we know from Jeremiah 29, God knows the plans He has for us.

We can also see from this story, that God delights in showing us grace even when we take things into our own hands. We know from the story in Genesis, that despite Sarah banishing Hagar and Ishmael into the desert, God was still with them. He provided Hagar and Ishmael water when they were on the brink of death.

It is comforting to know God's promises still fell on Ishmael even though his birth was the outcome of impatience with God's timing. God promised to make Ishmael into a great nation, (Genesis 21.18 NIV) even though he wasn't the fruit of God's promise to Abraham. Whilst the promise of a great nation and blessings of fruitfulness were on Ishmael's life, he was unable to benefit from having a covenant with God. A covenant relationship with God, was reserved for Isaac. (Genesis 17.19-22 NKJV)

The moments between the promise spoken and the promise coming to pass, can be a challenging, long and a character-building time. I do have to wonder, if sometimes we can delay the promise, by instigating events and circumstances, of our own design, to fast-track the waiting season.

As I mentioned, I have been single, for twenty long years. I didn't think it would be that long, as it was such a desire of my heart to be married.

In that time, there have been seasons of grace, of trusting and if I'm honest, of real frustration. There have been opportunities, to take matters into my own hands, again.

Thankfully, I am someone who learns from the consequences of my actions and doesn't tend to make the same choices again. The consequences of an unwise choice, outweigh the patient endurance, so I choose to wait. That's right. I need to choose that no matter how frustrated I get, I will not give in before my promise is here.

POSITION YOURSELF

There are ways we can position ourselves, to set ourselves up for a win. To position yourself action is required.

1 Samuel tells us the story of a beautiful woman named Hannah. Hannah's husband Elkanah had two wives, Hannah and Peninnah. Peninnah had children, but Hannah was unable to bear children. Peninnah used to love to throw this in Hannah's face.

It says in Chapter 1 of 1 Samuel, Peninnah would taunt and make fun of Hannah. This upset Hannah and she used to cry and would refuse to eat. Wow, some things sound not much different to the culture of today. (1 Samuel 1.6 NLT)

Have you ever felt less than, that you are not enough or had people make fun of you? Particularly if they have had the very thing your heart yearned for?

I think the enemy loves to wreak havoc with our minds in this area. Sometimes people's taunts can be obvious, and sometimes I wonder if the enemy whispers a lie, which take our minds on a spiralling tangent and make things bigger than they seem.

I have friends that have been unable to have children. They have shed the tears of disappointment, as they have compared themselves to the women who have many children and fallen pregnant easily. Pain upon pain enters their hearts, even just to walk into a shopping centre and see a new mother with a baby in a pram. I have heard their sobs, as their anguish spills over into one key question: 'Why can't it be me?' What makes matters worse, is when they see some women with multiple children, who for other reasons may not be able to take care of them. Often these children are given up for adoption or go to the foster system. When my dear friends, who so desire to have children of their own, watch this scenario play out in our society, it creates feelings of anger, jealousy and pain. Some things we won't understand this side of Heaven and then when we get there, God's loving perspective may even take these questions away. However right now the pain is very, very real.

One thing I do know, Hannah had a choice in this situation. Let's go on and see how Hannah positioned herself.

1. Church Community

Hannah went to the temple, or in today's language, church. She would cry and pray. It says Hannah was in deep anguish and cried bitterly as she prayed to the Lord. (1 Samuel 1.10 NLT)

I cannot express how passionate I am about the church of God. In a generation where some see the church as irrelevant in this modern era, I know it is relevant today and will be all the days of our life. In coming chapters I will go into further detail, around the importance of the body of Christ.

Each of us is 'in the waiting' for something, we are believing God for. It's a common theme for many. Whilst in the waiting, it is great to have people who help us stay accountable. To help us stay focused, stay the course and remain true to the promise yet fulfilled.

I intentionally position myself, by getting the right people around me. People to keep me accountable, to encourage me to wait patiently and who dare to believe greatly for the promise that's on its way, when to me it appears foggy and I've lost clarity.

These people are invaluable, and I'm sure they have wanted to hit me over the head at times, listening to my frustrations, seeing and hearing my tears and at times adult tantrums.

2. Prayer

Hannah didn't deny her emotions and her deep anguish and desire to have a child. She continued to pray and ask God to fulfil her heart's desire in giving her a child.

Eli the priest blessed her and said in verse 17 of chapter 1, *'Go in peace, may the God of Israel grant the request you have asked of Him.'*

Hannah responded with thanks and it says she began to eat and was no longer sad. In just two verses after what the priest had said, it says that the entire family got up early the next morning and went to worship the Lord.

Prayer is such a beautiful way we can converse with God. We have twenty-four seven access to the King of kings and the Lord of lords. To bring our requests to Him, to talk to Him, about anything and everything. He loves us to talk to Him.

Imagine if you lived in a house with someone, a significant other or even a flat mate. You wouldn't co-reside and not speak. Well, God is with us always and loves for us to speak to Him. Taking time to listen, like in any relationship, is always beneficial too. When we speak to God we can pray a formal prayer or you can speak to Him like you would a friend. After all He is the closet friend you'll ever have.

3. Worship

Worship is another way to position yourself. Have you ever had no words to even describe your heartache? I've heard so many people say, 'I couldn't even pray' or 'I had no words.' In these times I would encourage them to worship. Even if you can't sing, put on your favourite worship album and allow the music to wash over you. Even if the only position you can muster is being curled up, with no words coming out.

I have a reputation for my singing voice and it's all bad. I know I have trouble holding a tune, but there is something that happens in me when I worship. I cannot keep my hands down, up they go and yes, they tend to wave and move and the people who stand around me in church tend to move a few feet away, as they have been hit numerous times.

You know though, Sunday isn't the only day I worship. I worship every day. Intentionally in my daily quiet times, in my car and at work. (sorry guys) Worship is often on my lips and yes, in spite of the rough passage out, I know that God loves my worship, because it flows from my heart. It's part of my very being.

Worship changes something in you and in the atmosphere. It takes our focus off the situation and places it back onto God.

It goes on to say in that passage in chapter 1 that Hannah gave birth to a baby boy. She named him Samuel.

One thing I can tell you from my own story, is that God hears every cry of your heart and He sees every tear and His timing is always perfect, but not always in our sense of perfect, but it is all the same. Samuel wasn't only in Hannah's heart and desires, Samuel was in God's plan, as the miracle of Samuel wasn't just for Hannah, it was for Israel.

> Don't give up on positioning yourself well 'in the waiting' and don't let the promise become greater than the Promise Giver!

It's important that we don't make the promise, we are waiting and believing for with great expectation, bigger than the Promise Giver. Let the desire for God supersede your heart's desires.

When you're young and going on family vacation, often as a young person you are so excited to reach the destination. With a bored face and a few times after fighting with your sibling, you may hear from the parents in the front saying, 'enjoy the journey!'

So, enjoy the journey on the way to receiving your promise. God has given you everything you need to get through today. Every blessing, every spiritual gift, He has equipped you with all you need.

4. Praise

There are hundreds of verses in the Bible about praise.

'Bless the Lord O my soul and all that is within me bless His holy name.' (Psalm 103.1 NKJV)

'He is your praise and He is your God, who has done these great and awesome

things for which your eyes have seen.' (Deuteronomy 10.21 NKJV)

'Enter His gates with thanksgiving; into His courts with praise. Give thanks to Him and praise His name.' (Psalm 100.4 NLT)

'Praise the Lord! Oh, give thanks to the Lord, for He is good! For His mercy endures forever.' (Psalm 106.1 NKJV)

Praise changes atmospheres. If you are ever feeling down or overwhelmed and confused, grieving or have thoughts running around your head and you can't think straight, try praising as it changes your perspective. Similar to worship, it's taking your focus off your situation and putting it on to God.

> The Spirit of God is always
> with us in the waiting!

It's important that we know the character of God and not think that delay is punishment. He loves you; He sees you; He hears the yearning in your heart. He wants to draw us close to Himself in these times, not for us to draw away from Him.

I love that in the waiting we don't have to wait alone or in our own strength.

Romans 8.26-28, in The Message says, *'Meanwhile, the moment we get tired in the waiting, God's Spirit is right alongside helping us along. If we don't know how or what to pray, it doesn't matter. He does our praying in and for us, making prayer out of our wordless sighs, our aching groans. He knows us far better than we know ourselves, knows our pregnant condition and keeps us present before God. That's why we can be so sure that every detail in our lives of love for God is worked into something good.'*

We can grow tired in the waiting. It can be exhausting.
'So, let's not allow ourselves to get fatigued at doing good. At the right time we will harvest a good crop, if we don't give up or quit.' (Galatians 6.9 MSG)

Don't give up! I have seen so many people give up on their promise, when their promise was right around the corner. Thomas Fuller, an English theologian and historian has said this quote, which I love *'It's always darkest before the dawn.'*

God is always moving even when we don't see our circumstances move. He is working and making all the cogs move, ready for the promise.

One thing I know is that God is not one that He would dangle carrots, and He definitely isn't a cruel God.

> His delay is not a punishment to you.

God is working in our favour. He sees and moves on our behalf. He's moving in the unseen and the seen, aligning it all to bring these promises to fulfillment.

This is so true! We don't always see what He is doing but God is Alpha and Omega, the Beginning and the End. (Revelation 22.13)

We see the moment in front of us. When we wake up in the morning we don't know what the day will hold, but God does. He sees before the beginning of time, and He is not limited by time and He can also see the end. That's why trusting Him in the waiting is imperative. Trusting Him in every area is essential to living an abundant life.

THERE IS PURPOSE IN THE PAIN

We don't always understand the waiting time, especially if it's been a long time we've been waiting. There is always purpose in the pain of waiting. We may not understand why and that's okay.

When we position ourselves, we can help alleviate some of the pain and even bring it into a place of joyful expectation. The tools of being planted in a church community, prayer, worship and praise have the power to shift our perspective onto the Promise Giver. Looking into those eyes of love staring back at us can stir hope, peace and a sense of calm while we wait.

'I look up to the mountains – does my help come from there? My help comes from the Lord, who made Heaven and Earth! He will not let you stumble; the One who watches over you will not slumber. Indeed, He who watches over Israel never slumbers or sleeps. The Lord Himself watches over you! The Lord stands beside you as your protective shade. The sun will not harm you by day, nor the moon at night. The Lord keeps you from all harm and watches over your life. The Lord keeps watch over you as you come and go, both now and forever.' (Psalm 121 NLT)

Every season does pass. There are times and seasons for all things. *'To everything there is a season, a time for every purpose under Heaven: A time to be born, and a time to die; a time to plant and a time to pluck what is planted; a time to kill and a time to heal; a time to break down and a time to build up; a time to weep and a time to laugh, a time to mourn and a time to dance; a time to cast away stones and a time to gather stones; a time to embrace and a time to refrain from embracing; a time to gain and a time to lose; a time to keep and a time to throw away; a time to tear and a time to sew, a time to keep silence and a time to speak; a time to love and a time to hate; a time of war and a time of peace.'* (Ecclesiastes 3.1-8 NKJV)

The Promise Giver, the One who will never leave you or forsake you, is always developing something in you during the waiting that will set you up for your promise. Just like Joseph there may be gifts that require refining or practise in order for you to carry the fullness of your promise. If Joseph had not practised leadership, dream interpretation and service to others during his waiting time he may not have become the fair and wise ruler he was.

Some days may be one day at a time, others may be moment by moment. Ask God to reveal to you His purpose in the waiting. In asking God you may be able to see the gifts He has laid out for you whilst you wait. 'All things work together for good' and even the waiting can be used for good and can even set us up to receive the promise in full. What a wonderfully kind and compassionate God He is.

5. Thankfulness

I'm going to touch in more detail on thankfulness a bit later, but it is important in the waiting, to remain thankful and not get bitter. A bitter perspective can make the waiting more painful than it needs to be. Thankfulness on the other hand is essential to pain relief.

While you're waiting for your promise, remember all the amazing things in your life that you have. It's good to look at what we do have instead of what we don't have. Start small and begin thanking God for the things we often can take for granted, such as food in the pantry, clean water in the tap, or a dry place to sleep.

I encourage you today to be thankful. Before you go to bed tonight, thank God for three things that you are grateful for in your life. I guarantee it will change you, from the inside out.

WHAT IF THE PROMISE IS NOT FULFILLED?

In my prayers, I continue to declare and believe for my future husband. I also pray from time to time, 'Lord if I don't have my husband this side of Heaven, I will still always and forever worship You, thank You and believe that You are my husband.'

There needs to be a peace in your soul, that if your promise doesn't come to pass you will be okay. You are enough! You will get through this and live an abundant, full life.

As I said earlier, there are things that we don't understand. Why are some people healed and others not? Why can I not have children yet someone who has a dozen can? Why? Why? Why?

All I know, is His ways are higher than my ways. (Isaiah 55.8,9) Stay positioned, don't give up and keep your eyes on the Promise Giver.

This I do know, God is a good God. He wants what's best for us, beyond what we think we need and want. He knows all and sees all and IS ALL.

APP

- Where you are in your life today, is it where you dreamed and expected it would be?
- What disappointments do you have?
- What is something you can do positively, to deal with the disappointment you have experienced, to move forward and not allow disappointment to define you?

Chapter 3
Faith

'Now faith is the substance of things hoped for, the evidence of things not seen.'
(Hebrews 11.1 NKJV)

Since childhood I've had big faith. If God says it, I believe it. I do not need a theologian or a philosopher to give me the run down on the facts. I believe the Bible, and no one can deter me from believing what I believe about God, or that the bible is the inspired word of God.

Whilst I am open to learning and growing in new things, I am very strong in my faith in God and no one or nothing will tear me away from that. Faith according to an online dictionary is; *'confidence or trust in a person or thing,' 'Belief that is not based on proof' or 'belief in God or in the doctrines or teachings of religion.'*

Faith can be hard for some people to grasp. Some of my friends whose world view is factual, have struggled with faith as to them it's not something that can be defined in research or science. Faith, however, is something all people apply every day, if they have a belief in God or not. For example, we have faith that the weather report from the night before is correct. We have faith that we will go to bed each night and wake up in the morning. We place our faith in technology, in media reports, or other's 'expert' opinions. As humans, we are constantly gathering information to make informed choices and decisions. What most don't realise is that a component of making those decisions is often based on faith.

As Romans 4.16 (NLT) says, *'So the promise is received by faith. It is given as a free gift. And we are all certain to receive it, whether we live according to the law of Moses, if we have faith like Abraham's. For Abraham is the father of all who believe.'*

Faith is a gift, given freely. It is up to us whether we accept the gift and use it. It is also a different currency to the world's currency. Faith is believing before you see. There is a difference between facts or information-gathering and then God's perspective or God's truth about any given situation.

For example, you get a doctor's report which may be a fact and true. There is a diagnosis given. However, faith is declaring who God is in the situation. The higher truth is a gift offered in the form of faith. Believing God is the Healer and declaring 'I am healed', can often be the higher truth, even though there is a piece of paper with a fact written on it, which is also true.

Often times it can feel like you are holding two opposing views in these situations. You have a choice to accept the truth (fact) or place your focus on the truth and apply faith.

That being said, a diagnosis can be a very useful piece of information to help medical professionals and you understand methods and techniques that might remedy the impairment you may be facing. However, a diagnostic label is not where your identity lies in this situation.

I am not saying whether to use medicine or not here. Rather, I am saying no matter the circumstance we have a choice to believe what God says and who God says we are before believing what man or a piece of paper or a social media post says about us.

Personally, I want to have big faith like Abraham. To believe for things bigger than myself. To believe and have hope when all around me appears hopeless. There are a lot of verses in the Bible on faith. Some of my favourites are the following.

'But without faith it is impossible to please Him, for he who comes to God must believe that He is, and that He is a rewarder of those who diligently seek Him.' (Hebrews 11.6 NKJV)

'Jesus is the author and finisher of our faith.' (Hebrews 12.2 NKJV)

'So Jesus said to them, 'Because of your unbelief; for assuredly, I say to you, if you have faith as a mustard seed, you will say to this mountain, 'Move from here to there', and it will move; and nothing will be impossible for you.' (Matthew 17.20 NKJV)

To believe without seeing is a lot easier said than done. Are you a person who simply believes or do you need to have evidence and proof before you believe?

Our whole relationship with Jesus Christ is based on faith. To have an intimate relationship with someone we don't see, is well, I guess, odd to some people who don't have this relationship.

To those that do, it is not odd at all. It is a necessity. This relationship is one I don't ever want to live without, not for a fleeting second. Without Jesus, I would not be where I am today. He is the very foundation on which I stand.

People can look at our relationship as a crutch and to be honest that's okay. I don't need people's approval or opinion on my relationship with Jesus. I know He's real and that's all that matters to me.

What is important is putting faith at the forefront of our lives believing in things unseen. This not only has the power to change our life but the lives of those around us, including our children, grandchildren and great grandchildren. It's what some call a legacy of faith.

Let's look at two women in the Bible who had big faith and chose to say 'Yes' when it was scary. Their decisions cost them dearly, but their choice and the faith they exercised went on to bless entire generations.

The first is the story of the Widow at Zarephath. It's found in 1 Kings 17.8-24. To summarise this passage of scripture, God told Elijah to go to the town of Zarephath where there was a widow who would look after him. When Elijah got there, he asked the woman for food. She desperately expressed her desire to help, but also explained she could not, due to her lack of food for herself and for her child. Elijah asked her to take what she had and make bread anyway. He then went on to tell her to feed him first.

Imagine, this poor widow who didn't have enough bread to feed herself or her son, presented with the choice to feed a stranger or keep the small amount of food she had been storing, to save them from certain starvation. It seems like she had an opportunity to believe in the promises of God (the unseen realm) or plant her faith in the things she could see in the natural - a very small amount of flour and barely enough oil to make just one loaf of bread.

As we know from scripture, the widow did as Elijah asked. God blessed the widow's faith. True to His promises, He multiplied it, with the result that the widow and her son had food for much longer than made sense in the natural. If you read on, the scripture says the son dies. Elijah prays for this boy and he is healed and brought back to life.

What incredible blessings came from the strength of this widow's resolve. She placed her belief in God her Provider. In this story we can see the widow had faith for God to feed her beyond what she had in the natural. God met the widow's faith exactly where she was at. God was able to multiply the outcome above and beyond what was needed to sustain the small family using natural means.

> God never asks us for more than we have.
> He asks us to use what's in our hand.

He always meets us in our current circumstances, no matter how big or small our faith is. He will honour the smallest expression of faith and multiply it beyond our wildest dreams.

The second example is Mary. Mary had faith that God would do what He promised. In the culture of the time, being an unwed mother was a sure path to financial ruin, ridicule and a life of community exclusion. Mary made the choice to believe in the promises God had given her. She did it afraid, but she said 'Yes', and for generations to come, lives have been eternally changed. A legacy of faith and promise provided to all of humanity.

When I see Mary in Heaven I can't wait to give her my deepest gratitude. Mary's 'Yes' to God's promises and her courage to put her faith in things unseen, made way for the greatest gift the world has ever known.

BELIEVE

Proverbs 23.7 (NKJV) instructs us, *'For as he thinks in his heart, so is he.'*

There are so many factors that contribute to our personal belief systems. Our family of origin, our circumstances, trauma and words that have been spoken over us repeatedly. When we are at our lowest, feeling helpless or insecure, that is when our true belief, the things we hold true at our core, will surface.

Earlier, I spoke about 'Personal Truths.' This is something we believe to be true, but it is not the truth or Heaven's perspective.

For example, I shared that my personal truth was, I believed I was the ugliest person to ever walk the planet. This perception of myself affected my behaviour, my interactions with others, the relationship I had with myself and every other area of my life.

In my early teens, I would hate to be on my own. I would always have to be at a friend's house or have friends over at my house. The thought of being on my own terrified me. It wasn't because I was scared of people or the dark, however it was because I was living out of fear, to sit with my own thoughts and the hatred I had for myself, was a challenge I could not face.

Now at the time I wasn't aware of the reason why I needed to always have a friend over. It makes me so sad to know this is how I felt about myself.

> We behave and live our life out of what we believe.

The beauty in the heart of God was and is, that one prayer away, the One who designed me was at the ready to bring freedom into my life. I always had access to this freedom and to gain an understanding of who I was as a daughter of God. However, at that time, due to the wounds from my past and the lies I was believing about myself; I was unable to accept the gifts of freedom that God had purchased and already had in store for me.

Growing up, my amazing parents would tell me how beautiful I was. Dear older ladies in the church would affirm me as beautiful, however it didn't matter how many times I heard these words of kindness spoken over me. My heart could not agree with the word 'beautiful' because my personal truth was so contradictory. My personal filter was set in stone and could not be changed in my own strength.

Now, if someone said I was ugly, you bet I took that on. It reaffirmed what I already believed about myself. In the field of psychology this is called 'The Confirmation Bias.' Confirmation Bias is a term often used to describe how humans will search for and interpret information in a way that confirms their preconceptions. In my case, my preconception was that I was ugly. In a scientific application, this can lead to statistical errors when evaluating data. In a kingdom application, this can lead to believing the lies the enemy is whispering about our identity. In turn you seek to collect information that reinforces the lie rather that the truth of who God says we are in Him.

It was around twenty years ago when I first heard Ray Andrews, who is the International Director of NewLife World Wide Ministries. I have heard him speak and train multiple times. No matter how many times I listen to his teaching, I have found it extremely transformational and practical. (www.newlifewwm.com.au)

Over ten years ago, Ray came to our church and did some training. He said something I have never forgotten and have used it numerous times with people I've worked with.

He chose a young girl from the group and asked her how she'd feel if he called her a rabbit. Ray in his beautiful Irish manner was so sweet and reassured her she was a beautiful young lady, in a way only Ray can. The girl responded by shrugging her shoulders.

Ray then told us that if she didn't believe she was a rabbit, she wouldn't be upset by the comment and went on to demonstrate that we live out of what we believe.

If someone now says I'm ugly I can laugh it off. Today, I know who I am. I know that I'm not ugly and definitely not the ugliest person ever to walk the planet. I know that I am beautiful so the word 'ugly' no longer has the same effect it did when it was said to me at school for instance.

It's very important to search ourselves and see if we have any personal truths we are believing about ourselves, that are in fact lies.

When working with the people I've ministered to over the years, the most common personal truth they hold is, 'I am not enough.' From the time in the garden (Eden) the enemy has attacked people's identity. If he can get us doubting who we are, he can have a foothold. That's why it's so important we know who we are.

> First and foremost, before you are a mother, a wife, a teacher or anything else, YOU ARE A DAUGHTER OF THE MOST HIGH GOD! Everything else flows out of that.

When we have a revelation about our true identity in Christ, we will walk, think and ultimately live differently. Scripture tells us we live in authority. In Christ, authority has been given to us and we can live a life of abundance.

It needs to be a revelation, that we are everything He has said we are. Not labels that have been put on us, by others or by ourselves.

You are highly valued, far above rubies. There are so many scriptures, like this one, in the word of God, our manual for life, that are as relevant today as when they were written.

The word of God, the Bible, is our sword, the sword of the Spirit. We need to know the word of God through every fibre of our being. I am not just talking about memorising scripture, I am talking about sitting with a verse of scripture that strikes a chord in your heart. Allow that scripture to grow in your imagination. Think about how it makes you feel when you speak it over yourself. Draw a picture about it – really let it become a part of you. In doing this, when the enemy comes to tell you what you are or what you are not, that scripture will be able to cut through the enemy's lies with the precision of a surgeon, to declare the absolute truth.

Allowing scripture to become a part of us, as normal to us as breathing in and out, means we can use it with confidence and authority to respond with calm assurance when a lie presents itself.

I remember this beautiful older lady in our church who was a real grandma to so many of us younger mothers. She would invite us around for tea and scones, using her finest bone china. Beautiful memories of the older generation, pouring into the younger.

This lady oozed Jesus's love. She was so full of the word of God. She was always speaking life over us as young women.

This beautiful lady was diagnosed with an eye condition, where she could not see as clearly as she once could. Her vision had become impaired to the point she relied on a walking cane. I remember she shared that the saddest thing about this for her, was not going to be able to read her Bible. Tears rolled down her face. I took her by the hand and said, 'beautiful, you are so full of the word of God. You will always know it and live out of what is within you.' It was like an 'ah ha' moment for her. You know, when those wise things come out of your mouth – it must be the Holy Spirit, right?

We need to have the word of God in us. It is such a weapon against the fiery darts that come our way.

In Mark 9.23 (NKJV), Jesus says to a father wanting a breakthrough for his son, *'If you can believe, all things are possible to him who believes.'*

> All things are possible to YOU, dear one reading this book, if you believe.

When circumstances happen that are out of my control, where I need a breakthrough, I have taken a step back and asked myself, 'Who does God want to be for me in this moment?' For this father in Mark, chapter 9, God wanted to be his son's Healer and to be the father's Peace.

In every situation there is an opportunity to ask God 'Who do You want to be for me right now?' He is so faithful and always so kind to me in every situation. Like a loving father He is loyal and forgiving, wanting to hold me, and move on together, encouraging me on the way.

BUT WHO, ME?

I'm sure we've all had those occasions when we've had a 'Moses moment' and asked, 'Who me?' These are the times when we have not believed who we were or that we could do what God had assigned to us.

In Exodus 3, Moses is having the burning bush encounter with God. Verse 11 (NLT) says, *But Moses protested to God, "Who am I to appear before Pharaoh? Who am I to lead the people of Israel out of Egypt?"* Verse 12; *'God answered "I will be with you and this is your sign that I am the One who has sent you."*

Moses goes onto protest some more in regard to his inadequate knowledge and lack of polished communication skills. God reminded him of who He is. Verse 14 says, *"I Am Who I Am."*

Have you ever said, 'But God, who me?' I know I have. From a young age, I knew God had a plan for me, bigger than myself. Seeing visions and receiving prophesies on the plans He had for me was exciting yet scary. Often, I would say, 'God! but ...!'

I was sixteen years of age, the last time I asked 'why'? I had a conversation with God that challenged me to ask a different question, which settled my heart.

What if instead, I asked Him, 'Who do you want to be for me in this situation?' Or, 'What tool have you given me to get through this mountain?' Through, not around! I do not want to be a person that goes around and around the same mountain not learning a lesson.

When we have times of unbelief, it's then we need to remember who God is. We were not created to do life without Him. I Am Who I Am speaks of God who is self-sufficient, self-existent, all encompassing and without limitations. He is the only one in the universe who is not dependent on something else for His existence. (NLT commentary)

> God uses ordinary people to do extraordinary things.

Have you ever taken time to do an internal inventory on what you believe? It can be a very valuable exercise, because what we believe controls us.

Ask yourself firstly, what am I believing about myself and secondly, what am I believing about God in this moment? It's one thing to believe in God. Even the devil believes in God. It's different to believe God at His word. What the Bible says about who God is and who we are, can change us in the very depths of our heart.

HEART

'For as he thinks in his heart, so is he.' (Proverbs 23.7 NKJV)

What we believe in our heart is so important. I don't know if we realise how crucial this is. It effects our whole life.

We did a series on the heart at our women's group, at church. I heard stories of people having heart transplants who have taken on the person's belief systems, including their fears. For example, if someone received a heart from a person who was killed in a horrific accident, the heart recipient didn't understand why they would have overwhelming feelings of fear in certain situations. The heart recipient took on the beliefs and fears from the person they received the heart from.

What is in your heart? If you were to give someone your heart what would they experience?

How is the state of your heart? Are you holding offence or bitterness in your heart?

When I heard these stories of heart recipients it made me look at my heart and wonder what would happen if someone received my heart. Would it have been full of fear or was my heart a brave heart that was full of courage?

Luke 6.45 (NKJV) says, *'A good man out of the good treasure of his heart brings forth good; and an evil man out of the evil treasure of his heart brings forth evil. For out of the abundance of the heart his mouth speaks.'* Selah!

What do you talk about? They say you can tell the things that people find important if you take note of what they talk about. What's in your heart comes out your mouth in layman's terms. As I'm writing these pages, I'm challenging myself as well as you amazing readers.
Growing up I used to be told I was naïve. I would have this trusting

attitude that would see the good in everyone.

When I was in my first year of high school, I met this older man with additional needs, who used to catch the same bus. He was much older than my then twelve-year-old self, possibly around forty. He was so friendly and nice, and I was one of the only young people who would be nice to him and talk to him. He asked me to his house one day and being a rule keeper, I said I would need to ask my parents.

When I asked my parents, they of course said 'no.' They tried to help me by giving me the reasons why not, but I just thought they were being mean. I told him 'no' and he was so sad, which made me angrier at my parents.

This is an extreme example, however it has been a common theme throughout my life. I would have empathy for people, sometimes pity being the motive over my own safety. I have learnt, from hard lessons in life, to guard my heart when showing empathy to others.

We are encouraged in Proverbs 4.23 (NLT); *'Guard your heart above all else, for it determines the course of your life.'*

What a powerful encouragement. True words of wisdom.

I love Dr Phil, and in a lot of his shows says we often trust people too easily. He implores us that people need to earn our trust and to watch out for red flags. He said, *'It's better to be alone and healthy than sick with someone else.'*

Now, I'm not by any means suggesting we walk around with six-foot walls around our hearts. There is however a fine line between having walls and being wise and guarding our hearts.

Boundaries are a God designed idea. From the Garden of Eden, in Genesis, God had boundaries. He told Adam and Eve what they could eat and what they could not. Boundaries are always for safety and for our better good. What does it look like to guard your heart?

When we first begin setting boundaries, often solid walls are what we feel are needed to protect ourselves. However, I have learnt there are other ways to live free, yet all the while guarding my heart.

Asking God for His wisdom and help to guard my heart is always my first step. He knows all, is Alpha and Omega, sees all, knows every motive and every thought.

In the Bible it says, numerous times, that Jesus saw the hearts of the people He was speaking to, often referring to the Pharisees. Jesus would hear them speak, but always looked at the heart motive behind what they were saying. I think we can take this example and apply it when guarding our hearts.

We often only see what a person wants us to see.

A person can be stylishly dressed, have the nicest words and appear to be doing all the right things, yet something just doesn't add up. We may be discerning or listening to that 'gut feeling' and then, after some time, their true colours show.

I'm sure we all know people like this and can recount times in our own lives where a person's behaviour behind closed doors, is contrary to their words and actions in the public arena.

Matthew 10 tells the story of Jesus sending out the twelve apostles. In verse 16 (NKJV) Jesus says, *'Behold, I send you out as sheep in the midst of wolves. Therefore, be wise as serpents and harmless as doves.'*

As Christians, some of us have believed a lie that we need to be doormats. Nowhere in scripture do I see Jesus being a doormat. I see

Him walk in love, love like no other, but never did He allow Himself to be abused, excluding when He chose to go to the cross, with the purpose that we would never be separated from God again.

I am a sheep. We work with and live in a world full of people who can be sheep or wolves and even wolves in sheep's clothing. We are sheep but God wants us to live as wise as serpents and harmless as doves.

A minister in our church and friend of mine explains this verse this way; *'We are to live as cunning as the devil and as innocent as the Holy Spirit.'* (David Balestri) We don't need to be intimidated by wolves. We can be wise as serpents.

Apparently, most snakes do not see well. Generally, they can see shapes but not details. They have pits on the side of their head to sense heat (infrared light) like night vision goggles. These pits, not eyes, actually are said to give the snake an image, in their brains of their prey.

We don't have pits on the side of our head, but we can test the atmosphere and have discernment with the power of the Holy Spirit.

As Christ followers, when we are in our workplace, our shopping centre, our home or our church, can taste the air, not with our natural eyes but with our spiritual eyes.

Gentle or innocent as doves. We can be gentle, innocent and look at people through Jesus's lens. This means we can also be wise, aware, careful, enlightened, well informed, perceptive, smart and sensible all at the same time.

When an unsafe person comes into your world or sphere, that looks right (looks like a sheep/Christian) and acts right, (like a sheep/Christian) we have the Holy Spirit to help us be all these things I've just mentioned above and to discern whether they are safe or unsafe. Then we can respond appropriately, in love, as Christ would and with appropriate strategies.

Another way to help guard my heart is gather outside perspectives from a trusted confidant.

Interestingly, we can all manipulate a scripture, a prophetic word or a situation and twist it to suit our own needs and desires.

Just recently I was confused about a situation in my life and had lots of voices offering well-meaning advice. However, something felt a little off. So, I phoned a dear trusted, prophetic friend, and she helped me have clarity and, in actual fact reminded me of what I already actually knew. I was just doubting because of the noise going on around the situation.

It's important to have a trusted posse around you, to help you guard your heart on the big issues of life, especially when we lose perspective. Our heart is something we can choose to treasure and look after well. Guard what goes in, as it effects what flows out.

It says in Psalm 34.18 (NLT), *'The Lord is close to the broken hearted; He rescues those whose spirits are crushed.'*

God is the one who can mend our broken heart and make it like new again. Only God, not people, or things, only Him. Let's do a health check on the state of our hearts today. Spend some time reflecting on what is in your heart.

APP

- What do you believe? Who does God want to be for you in this season you're in?
- Is there a personal truth you are believing about yourself, that may be a lie?
- Are you not believing God can meet a need in your life?

Chapter 4

Intentional living

'So be very careful how you live, not being like those with no understanding, but live honourably with true wisdom, for we are living in evil times. Take full advantage of every day as you spend your life for His purposes.'
(Ephesians 5.15,16 TPT)

As I journey through my life, the more I realise it is crucial to be intentional. All of us were born on purpose, with great purpose and for this time in history. Intentionality flows out of knowing we were born on purpose. Our time, money and relationships can all have the principal of intentionality added to them.

What we allow in and out of our life, can at times, feel overwhelming. We can busy ourselves with so many activities and commitments. Weeks turn into months, months turn into years and we catch ourselves saying, 'where did the time go?'

We all have twenty-four hours in the day, and we are stewards over our lives. Wow! That's a big statement with a lot of responsibility.

Our choices are key to making intentionality a cornerstone life principle. We can choose to meander through life or apply thought, value and consciousness to the way we think and act.

We cannot place blame on anyone or anything for how we choose to live our lives. The choices we make are ours alone. When we assign blame to others or circumstances we are choosing to allow people or events to dictate the present, and in turn, determine our future steps.

As I mentioned earlier, there are also circumstances that have happened to us. Some are due to choices we have not made ourselves. However, with intentionality we have the opportunity to choose our next steps wisely, opening up the possibility to change the future course of our lives.

The choice is mine! That is a very empowering statement. The choice is mine! Selah!

INTEGRITY

Earlier I mentioned about values. One of my top five is integrity.

Integrity is 'the quality of being honest and having strong moral principles that you refuse to change.' (dictionary.cambridge.org/amp/english/integrity) Integrity is doing the right thing, even when people are not watching.

Most of us would think that stealing from a shop or from a place of work, does not demonstrate a strong moral compass. This may sound a little extreme but what about being late to work or finishing earlier and fudging a little on your timesheet. Is this ok? Everybody does it right? As Christians, integrity should be a natural part of our character. To be a Christian means being a Christ follower. When we look at the life of Christ, it is clear that He was the most integrous person who ever walked the planet. When we partner in unity with the Holy Spirit, integrity can naturally flow from our character. The gift of integrity is ours and is freely offered to us in abundance.

EAR AND EYE GATE

With integrity in mind, it is of utmost importance to be mindful of what we allow to come into our life.

Our ears and eyes take in millions of pieces of data. It is clear we live in a golden age of information. Some information that floats around us is not always true and is not always good for us. Other information is edifying and can propel us forward. When we are taking in information we can stop and consider what we are allowing through these gateways Is it wisdom? Is it true? Does it reinforce negative thinking?

> You are the gate keeper, so be intentional with what you allow to pass.

Over the years, I have copped many laughs and misunderstanding over the types of movies I choose to watch, or should I say choose not to watch. I have been known to walk out of movie theatres and leave lounge rooms while people are watching things I know are not good for me to engage in. I do this because I am very careful about what I allow through my gateways.

Being very visual, I made it a standard that I won't watch movies and television shows with explicit sex scenes. In this day and age it is quite hard to find things to watch without overt and very physical sex scenes. Whilst this may not be a standard for everyone, it is one I hold myself to and I know it benefits my life immensely.

Now I understand we all have our own convictions and standards in our lives. Please understand, I am not trying to say everyone needs to have the same as mine. I do however want to remind us all that we are responsible for what we allow in. Only you can answer what is good for your soul to hear and see. The Holy Spirit is so kind and generous in the outpouring of wisdom over our lives. A simple request for wisdom from the Holy Spirit will help you discern what is right and good for your soul.

Money

Money is such an essential part of our world. Now I'm sure there are people reading this that wish they had more money so they could be intentional with it. Again ... Choices ...

Have you ever taken an intentional look at your bank account? Horrified, is an understatement when I saw how many take away and food transactions, I noticed on my bank statement, one month.

A good way to see areas of priority in our life is take note of what we spend our money on. We will all have different budgets, bills, debts and other financial commitments.

A key principal I apply to my finances is allocating a portion that goes to tithe first. Bills, household expenses, savings and spending all flow from the remainder of my financial allocation.

Now, I understand every person reading this will have different obligations and priorities. You may also have different feelings towards tithing or not quite understood tithing as a key life principal.

When we understand God's economy we will come to learn where a commandment is given, a blessing is attached. My life is a true testament to following God's economic principals. Countless times I have experienced financial blessing simply by committing to giving a portion of my income back to God.

Jesus demonstrated extravagance to me by laying down His life, so I could live in abundance. This true demonstration of love is another reason why I give my tithe into my local church.

Anything I want to give on top is an offering. My tithe belongs to the church, in which I'm planted.

'Glorify God with all your wealth, honouring Him with your very best, with every increase that comes to you. Then every dimension of your life will overflow with blessings from an uncontainable joy!' (Proverbs 3.9,10 TPT)

Stewarding money takes a lifetime of practice. I have found this to be true in my own life. To be intentional with where my money goes and invest my seed into kingdom endeavours, continues to be a great adventure. Not just with my tithe, but as it says in the scripture from Proverbs above, with all my wealth. I take each step with the Holy Spirt and delight as I see Kingdom exchanges and abundant miracles.

ABIDE

Abide: 'to remain; continue; stay.' (Dictionary.com)

I love chapter fifteen in the book of John. This is Jesus speaking. In one passage Jesus says abide seven times:

'I am the true vine, and My Father is the vinedresser. Every branch in Me that does not bear fruit He takes away; and every branch that bears fruit He prunes, that it may bear more fruit. You are already clean because of the word which I have spoken to you. Abide in Me, and I in you. As the branch cannot bear fruit of itself, unless it abides in the vine, neither can you, unless you abide in Me. I am the vine; you are the branches. He who abides in Me, and I in him, bears much fruit; for without Me you can do nothing. If anyone does not abide in Me, he is cast out as a branch and is withered; and they gather them and throw them into the fire, and they are burned. If you abide in Me and My words abide in you, you will ask what you desire, and it shall be done for you. By this My Father is glorified, that you bear much fruit; so, you will be My disciples.' (John 15.1-8 NKJV)

The Greek meaning of abide is to *remain, tarry, not to depart, to continue to be present, to be held, kept, continually, endure, to survive and to live.* (Biblestudytools.com)

Have you ever noticed how we tend to take on the idiosyncrasies of the people we spend the most time with? I'm sure you've heard the famous Jim Rohn quote; *'You're the average of the five people you spend the most time with.'* (developgoodhabits.com)

This quote is also true when we prioritise our greatest relationship. The one we have with Jesus. If we abide in Him and He in us, we cannot help but take on the idiosyncrasies of the character of God and the fruits of the Holy Spirit. I wonder what it would be like if we started living our lives flowing from love, joy, peace, patience, kindness, goodness, faithfulness, gentleness and self-control? (Galatians 5) Dwelling and abiding means continually relying on God in every area of our lives.

When I'm in worship, devotion and reflective times, dwelling and abiding comes easily. However, when I'm around people and some certain personalities that rub me the wrong way, abiding becomes much more of a challenge. We have all experienced these moments. Some people and life circumstances have the tendency to trigger old patterns of self-protection. Our 'fight or flight' response is activated and before we know it, we are reacting out of a wounded place.

It is in these circumstances, when the 'fight or flight' is activated, we have the choice to actively abide in the Holy Spirit. I say actively because it may not flow as easily as when we are in worship or reflective times. Abiding is a gift on offer from the heart of God. In most circumstances it is a way to sooth an intense emotion or a heartache from a past wounding. When I abide in Him, I am resting in Him. A branch doesn't hang there stressing about pushing out fruit or leaves. It hangs with complete reliance on the source of the tree or vine.

'Since I began a relationship with Jesus, He grafted me into Himself. I stay there through faith or I can stop abiding and close the door by pride and unbelief.' (Ray Andrews - Newlife World Wide Ministries)

For example, I go out to start my day after I've had an amazing time of devotion. I run into a person who is less than personable and is quite rude and starts yelling at me. I have a choice in that moment to stay in that place of rest and remain abiding or to start yelling back and reacting. As quickly as I disconnect from the vine I can go back to abiding. I have learnt to ask myself what am I believing about myself right now? Am I feeling unsafe?

As I mentioned earlier my number one need, due to my temperament, is security. If my security is threatened, in any way, I need to be conscious of not going into defence mode. The reason I do this, is there is something I'm believing that God can't meet in that moment, therefore I go into my own strength to do all I can to make myself feel secure.

When I disconnect from the vine, it doesn't take long until that little branch or cutting can no longer survive without the source of the vine. Unlike a cutting in nature, you and I can make a simple choice, time and time again, to reattach to that precious life source.

The NewLife training I learnt on abiding was invaluable to me. When I learnt about myself, and about my temperament, I had a greater understanding of who God wanted to be for me in each and every moment. I learnt to abide and the ease that is on offer for me to enjoy. Even when I step away from the vine, I know I am only ever one choice away from taking solace in rest and ease. Life-changing!

Sometimes, life is one day at a time sweet Jesus, other times it's moment by moment.

When we abide in Christ, we will in turn produce fruit. Fruit that displays Christ. I want to reveal beautiful attributes of Jesus.

> Imagine if people didn't know where
> Jesus and I ended because we were
> so intertwined together. Selah!

BEING THE CHEERLEADER OF YOUR OWN LIFE

Cheering other people on in life, is something I am very passionate about. Encouraging others is something that is quite natural to me. Encouraging and cheering myself on however, has been a journey in and of itself.

At the moment, a friend of mine and I are choosing healthy eating habits. We are doing the same food regime and encouraging one another and staying accountable to each other.

Yesterday we were both having a day where we had a little, sweet treat. As anyone working with making conscious food choices knows, emotions can be heavily linked to food. My dear friend revealed to me that the one sweet treat she had consumed had put her on a downward spiral. I found it easy to encourage my friend. A confident, 'Okay honey you've eaten one thing, let's turn and start the day again and choose to nourish for the rest of the day,' easily fell from my lips.

Saying this to my friend was so easy and natural. I was at the same time internally saying to myself, 'Well you've busted, and may as well keep eating junk today and start again tomorrow,' in my harshest critical voice. Being a cheerleader in my own life is something I need to be reminded of and intentional about choosing to do.

Now David was greatly distressed, for the people spoke of stoning him, because the soul of all the people was grieved, every man for his sons and his daughters. But David strengthened himself in the LORD his God.' (1 Samuel 30.6 NKJV)

To have people in your world that are encouraging and cheer you on is priceless. We do need to learn to do this for ourselves too. So many times, in life, I've heard people struggle with not being recognised or feel they haven't been heard or seen for their service or for other things they've done.

Have you ever been celebrated? There are many ways you can celebrate someone. By throwing them a party in their honour or to say something nice about the person. When I've been celebrated, I've felt so valued, honoured and respected. It puts a bounce in my step.

Now while this is great, I don't want to live from a place of only feeling valued when I am being celebrated by others. I want to celebrate, encourage and cheer myself on, every day and know I am doing what I am doing in life, because I have purpose and because I have the backing of God.

Value isn't a feeling. It's part of who I am. I am valued!

Wanting praise and to be celebrated by others can come back to temperament. Some people crave praise and recognition. This is something we really need to keep tabs on ourselves. If we require this from people for everything we do, we may need to ask Holy Spirit why that is?

'Do your best. Work from the heart for your real Master, for God, confident that you'll get paid in full when you come into your inheritance. Keep in mind always that the ultimate Master you're serving is Christ.' Colossians 3.23. (MSG)

We need to give ourselves an attitude assessment every now and then.

How do I respond if my husband or wife, my employee, or my pastor doesn't recognise all the hard work I'm doing? Do I get bitter, or think what an ungrateful so and so? Why are you doing what you are doing?

If it is only for recognition, power and prestige, maybe it's time you asked yourself what is lacking in you? Is there a gap or an unmet need that keeps surfacing? I wonder what that need might be?

We all have a 'God-shaped' hole in us, that only God can fill. Often, we look at different ways we can fill this void ourselves. Recognition can be one way. Unfortunately, when we strive for recognition rather than allowing God to meet this need through abiding, the result is pride and unbelief.

What are you not believing about who God is for you in that moment?

Learn to encourage and cheer yourself on. Every morning, you could intentionally wake up and say something like, 'Today I am equipped and empowered to do all I need to do and it's going to be a great day.' That right there will give you an attitude adjustment. Then if at work, or wherever you are, you see someone else get recognition, you can smile and truly be happy for them, and not devalue yourself, as you can live from a place of being whole.

I've often wondered why we, the body of Christ, struggle with something called 'tall poppy syndrome'.

'Tall poppy syndrome describes aspects of a culture where people of high status are resented, attacked, cut down, strung up or criticised because they have been classified as superior to their peers. The term has been used in cultures of the English-speaking world.' (Wikipedia)

My heart has been broken from some of my observations of 'tall poppy' behaviour in the body of Christ. Tearing down brothers and sisters purely because of a perceived level of greatness, is far from the character of Christ. It happens nonetheless, with devastating consequences.

We are all on this Earth to ultimately do the same thing, which is bringing glory to God. We are uniquely created to display different facets of God to our world. Let's be intentional by speaking words of life over one another, not being like the enemy, the 'accuser' of the brethren. (Revelation 12.10)

When we realise this, we will be comfortable in our own skin, stop tearing others down, not compete with others and run in our own lane.

RUNNING IN YOUR OWN LANE

You were only ever meant to be YOU!

I was not created, formed so preciously in my mother's womb to be and fulfil the call of Queen Elizabeth II. I was created to be me.

That should be so freeing to know. There is peace in knowing, all I have to be is ME. We can take the pressure off ourselves and stop comparing ourselves with one another.

> I am called to be me, and ultimately use the gifts and talents God has given me and fulfil all He has called me to do.

The more I practice the principals of abiding, the more comfortable I am in my own skin. I've intentionally invested time to discover who I already am and then allowed God to meet me with His blueprint for my life. Allowing Him to reveal who He wants to be for me in each moment strengthens my enjoyment of who I am. When I submit those parts I have perceived were weaknesses, I understand that God made me this way to fulfil my purpose. I am 'strong-willed' because I am passionate to advocate for what is right. This takes courage and strong resolve which others might call 'stubbornness.' With this in mind I can stay in my own lane. I don't need to compare myself with others because I was made this way on purpose.

In an Olympic athletics event, the competitors all run in the same direction, with the same rules and guidelines, with the same lane width, all keeping their eyes on the prize of winning the race.

If a runner goes into the lane of the person next to them, they are disqualified. The game is over for them.

Have you ever seen that happen? A runner may have lost their footing or gone too wide and stepped over. There can be damage done if they run into the other runner and they can both be hurt.

In life, how liberating would it be, if there was no more competing and comparing our lives to others and trying to tear people down? It would look pretty good if you ask me. We can't control what others do, but what we can do, is choose to step out of the world of competing and comparing.

We may see someone excelling and think how did they get to where they are? Firstly, we don't know their story, of how they got to where they are today. Secondly, we don't know the sacrifice they have put in to get to where they are today. We only see the here and now or their 'highlight reel.'

Today, I am a confident woman who holds her head up high, who is a pastor in a thriving church, an online campus pastor who speaks to people every Sunday from across the street and around the globe. People don't know what I've gone through (well you all do now by reading this book) to get to here. Likewise, we don't know what others have done in their life, so let's take the pressure off right here and now. Repeat after me, 'I'm free to be me!'

To do life in your own lane, you don't need to look at how the person next to you is running, you need to focus on the finish line, whilst maintaining your breathing and stride.

> The only person you should compare yourself to is you!

There are benchmarks I set for myself. I use these to compare how well I was doing last week or last month. I don't need to compare myself to how well the friend next to me executes that same thing.

Once a month a friend and I go to 'weigh in.' We encourage one another in our progress. We don't compare our wins and losses with each other. We only compare our results to our own previous results, whilst cheering each other on along the way.

Comparison is ugly. It causes disappointment and sadness. We all have been given what we need, to do what God has called us to do.

'God has given each of you a gift from His great variety of spiritual gifts. Use them well to serve one another.' (1 Peter 4.10 NLT)

I don't need to measure my gift to my brother. I need to use the gift God has given me to fulfil why I've been put on the Earth. Doesn't that take a load off?

In the body of Christ, we are unique, different parts making up one body.

1 Corinthians 12.14-22 (NLT) says, *'Yes, the body has many different parts, not just one part. If the foot says, "I am not a part of the body because I am not a hand," that does not make it any less a part of the body. And if the ear says, "I*

am not part of the body because I am not an eye," would that make it any less a part of the body? If the whole body were an eye, how would you hear? Or if your whole body were an ear, how would you smell anything? But our bodies have many parts, and God has put each part just where he wants it. How strange a body would be if it had only one part! Yes, there are many parts, but only one body. The eye can never say to the hand, "I don't need you." The head can't say to the feet, "I don't need you." In fact, some parts of the body that seem weakest and least important are actually the most necessary. And the parts we regard as less honourable are those we clothe with the greatest care.'

It goes on, in verse 25, to say that when we work together, it makes for harmony. If one part hurts, we all hurt. We shouldn't need to push each other out of our own lanes. We all have a different part to play.

If I had to lead our church family in worship this Sunday, let me tell you, it wouldn't be long until the building was cleared. However, when I talk to people, help people connect, lead teams and be present with the one in front of me, I know I am working with the gifts God has given to me. I leave the worship leading to the ones that are gifted in that area.

If we only had worship in church, there would be something missing too. We need the pastor preaching, we need the person welcoming at the door, the kids' team and the person who restocks the toilet paper. No one is any more important than the other. We all need each other and when we understand that and treat each other accordingly, our world will be a better place

Growing up I used to compare myself to my brother. I thought when God gave out talents he got excess and I didn't seem to get any.

My brother, being very creative could draw, pick up any musical instrument and play by ear, could sing like a beautiful song bird and would often from a church platform to a concert of hundreds get compliments, standing ovations and make my parents so very proud.

In my twenties I realised (through others pointing them out) that my talents were connecting, loving people, showing empathy, listening, empowering and placing dignity on people.

It is very important to understand we all have been given talents and gifts, that may look different to your loved ones.

SELF-CARE

Nearly ten years ago I completed chaplaincy training. I learnt so many valuable lessons through this course with one of the main take-aways being self-care.

With life in general, we tend to live in the fast lane, going at a pace of one hundred miles an hour, with the hustle and bustle to keep in the flow. Family, work, extracurricula activities, social time and the list goes on.

Do you ever feel like you are so busy doing, that there's no time to 'be?' Do you intentionally incorporate self-care into your world?

It's so easy to look after everyone in our world, whether that be our significant other, children, parents or friends. Often, it is harder to prioritise looking after ourselves. We can only give out from a position of overflow.

I remember years ago, travelling with my then, small child and hearing the safety announcement as the plane was taking off.

The air hostess informed us if you are travelling with a child and there is an emergency, be sure to place the oxygen mask on yourself before your child.
The thought that went through my mind at that moment was 'as if I would save myself before my child.' If you are a parent, you know you love your precious children more than life itself.

It wasn't until I did this chaplaincy training and the Lord really spoke to me about caring for myself as much as I did for other people in my world. (Similar principals to the cheering on, earlier in this chapter)

Learning this was imperative to my own life and then coaching and pastoring others on how to do this well too. If you are continually running on empty, how long do you think you can keep going until something gives way? It may be your health or even lead to burnout.

> We can't give out from an empty cup. It is of utmost importance, in life, to prioritise self-care.

What if I told you that looking after yourself, would in turn lead to you being a better person to those around you? We at times think we are invincible. However, if we aren't looking after ourselves something will eventually give. You can't keep running a car on empty. You have to fill it with petrol and make sure the oil and tyres are good and give it a service regularly. Why then are we so less likely to nurture our own body and soul?

Understanding that most people live big lives, there are so many ways to incorporate self-care. First, ask yourself what nourishes your soul?

Some things I love to do is to go to a cafe and have coffee with a friend or sit at the beach. There is something so refreshing for my soul sitting by the ocean, watching sunrises, sunsets and gazing at the stars.

Once a month I have a day put aside where I have a self-care day. It is a day where I have extended time with God. I will go and have coffee at my favourite coffee shop, sit by the beach, write in my journal and chill. My phone is off, and I am uncontactable for a few hours, and it is absolute heaven.

Then, a few times a week, I go and sit at the beach or go and watch a sunrise or sunset. There are endless things you can do to look after you. After all, you cannot keep running on low. So how are you going to fill your cup today?

APP

- Spend some time with Holy Spirit and journaling around the areas of integrity and your ear and eye gates.
- Spend some time with Holy Spirit around 'Abiding.' See what He reveals to you around unbelief and pride where you do things in your own strength. Get your journal and pen ready.
- How can you intentionally cheer yourself on in an area of your life?

Chapter 5

Give Yourself Permission

'Our deepest fear is not that we are inadequate. Our deepest fear is that we are powerful beyond measure. It is our light, not our darkness that most frightens us. We ask ourselves, 'Who am I to be brilliant, gorgeous, talented, fabulous?' Actually, who are you not to be? You are a child of God. Your playing small does not serve the world. There is nothing enlightened about shrinking so that other people won't feel insecure around you. We are all meant to shine, as children do. We were born to make manifest the glory of God that is within us. It's not just in some of us; it's in everyone. And as we let our own light shine, we unconsciously give other people permission to do the same. As we are liberated from our own fear, our presence automatically liberates others.'
(Marianne Williamson)

This is my favourite quote. We need to give ourselves permission. Permission to shine, to excel and to dream, bigger and beyond ourselves.

I don't know what your family of origin is, I don't know if people in your family or significant others in your life have gone on to live big lives, but I want to tell you, that when you give yourself permission in life to live an extraordinary life, you will excel.

You may be the first in your family or in your circle of friends to live a 'big life,' and that will take bravery. I want to, right here and right now, inject a huge 'YOU CAN DO IT!' Those first shaky but determined steps towards your 'big life' can feel daunting. Rest assured anything you put your mind to, you can do.

> *'If you can dream it, you can do it.'*
> Walt Disney

Often, we are waiting for permission from our significant others, our bosses or our peers to do something before taking action. Really, what we need to do is back ourselves and do it.

Now, in saying this, I'm referring to a personal dream or goal. Of course, in marriage or a place of employment, we need to discuss taking action with the relevant people our dreams or goals will impact.

At school my mum would sign a permission slip to allow me to go on an excursion or school camp. My Mum's signature gave me permission to go. It held authority. We have permission in our own lives to be the best version of ourselves that we can be.

Are you waiting for permission to do what you already have the authority to do?

That is a great question to ask ourselves, regularly.

Often fear is the reason we don't give ourselves permission to live our greatest lives. What are you afraid of? What's holding you back from living your best life?

Fear of:

failure	the unknown	rejection
not being enough	people's expectations	other people's opinions
change	not being in control	the cost or sacrifice
missing out	lack	loneliness
uncertainty	being judged	losing freedom

Fear is such a huge life limiter. If we give fear the reigns, it can choke us and hold us back from entering our best life. If we give fear the power, it can wreak havoc.

It's great to be aware of the fears we have and name them. In naming our fears, we can give ourselves permission to soften the harsh edges around these thought constructs, and work towards dissolving our fears all together.

Each time a fear edge is softened we move forward into our purpose and all we are designed to fulfil in our life.

1 John 4.18 (NKJV) says, *'There is no fear in love; but perfect love casts out fear, because fear involves torment. But he who fears has not been made perfect in love.'*

> We have permission, from Heaven, to walk as mature, yes mature, sons and daughters of God.

Permission granted! I want to stamp that over your life today, in big bold black ink! You have permission to be you!

Years ago, I was going through an emotional season. Things in my home were out of control and I did not feel I had any power to make change. As much as I wanted the other people around me to change, I've learnt we can only change ourselves, not others.

It was a scary, sad, traumatic season, that brought many triggers, much stress and anxious thoughts. It's very difficult to live with little, or no control. Especially when that loss of control is going on in your home. Home is a place that should be safe and peaceful.

A beautiful friend of mine was travelling from her home, five hours away, to a nearby city so we planned to meet up on her way through. As soon as she saw me, she could tell I wasn't in a great place. She asked me what was going on and I shared the last year, that seemed to be all-consuming and very stressful.

I don't remember everything she said to me, in that one hour catch up. However, one thing spoken will stay with me forever. It was like a tender nudge, to remind me what and who I am.

She spoke God's perspective into my life.

She said something like this ... 'Kylie, you were called to be a mother. Of course, that's the area that the enemy wants to attack, because it's the very thing you're called to be.'

Right then and there, in the restaurant, noise all around, Jesus started talking to my heart, so tenderly. He reminded me of when I was born, and the doctors were saying I wouldn't live. A beautiful lady in our church gave my parents a word saying, 'Kylie will be a mother to Israel.' Those words given by God through the lady in our church ring true today more than ever. I was born to be a mother, not just to my offspring but to many others, so of course, as my precious friend said, that is the very thing that the enemy came to steal.

When I was born, the expert opinion of doctors tried to take all permission away from me to thrive and succeed. God had His way and did what only God can. He said 'Live' and here I sit, writing to you today.

In both of these instances, I had a choice. A choice on whether to give myself permission to live a flourishing life, or to let others or my circumstances dictate my choices. Anyone who knows me knows that I chose the former.

The world and culture in which we live, would have given me permission to sit back and live a life, not expecting much out of myself. However, I choose to live out of God's perspective and the daily encouragement He gives me. I know I don't have to live a life according to what others think and perceive me to be.

Have people, maybe even people you love, or the enemy, tried to steal your permission?

In John 10.10 (NIV) Jesus says, *'The thief comes only to steal and kill and destroy; I have come that they may have life and have it to the full.'*

> The enemy can only kill and destroy what we allow him to steal

It is time to take back our permission, to reclaim what the enemy has stolen. It's never too late. It's time to give ourselves permission, that was already ours, to have life and to live it to the full. Selah!

When you give yourself permission to be you, some people may be intimidated, but remember, that is their issue, not yours. When we are confident and can hold our heads high, it can do one of two things. It can reveal greatness or brokenness in others around us. It will either pull people up or they will feel put down. The choice is theirs.

As we walk in agreement of what is ours to possess, it is our hope that it unlocks greatness in those around us. Many of us have built walls around ourselves. I know when I came out of that toxic relationship, I swore no one would ever hurt me like that, or control me ever again. I didn't realise at the time that I'd built six-foot walls around myself. While I healed they served a purpose. They kept me safe and kept others at bay. Walls do serve a purpose. Walls keep others out, but they also keep us contained.

As you are reading this, some of you know it's time to give yourselves permission to smash those walls. I see you with a big sledgehammer, smashing brick walls that have been around you for a very long time. You are laughing and you look strong and free, ready to break free from those walls. Whilst they may have served a purpose in the past, they don't serve you anymore. You are ready!

There are many areas we can give ourselves permission in.

Permission to:

look after you	step out	be successful
be imperfect	enjoy singleness	drop the walls
dream big	be happy	love and be loved
be free	break cycles	be present
say 'no'	say 'yes'	be your authentic self
live fearless	ask for help	leave the past behind
put in boundaries	allow yourself to feel	leave excuses behind
not sweat the small stuff	face your fear	do it afraid
surrender to the process	heal	live your best life
unfollow on social media	don't be controlled	refuse comparison
be your own hero	be content	celebrate the wins

Whatever season of life you are in right now, whether you're a stay-at-home mum, a career person, an entrepreneur, a nurse or executive, give yourself permission to be you, in the season you're in right now. There is purpose in the moment you're in.

One of my closest friends is in her baby season and it was a big adjustment from being a very accomplished career woman. Obviously, with any new parent, it's a big season of going from where you have prestige and in a place of power and influence, to then going to a season, as rewarding as it can be, to wiping dirty hands, faces and bottoms, with little to no thanks.

In these very seasons of life there is purpose. There are opportunities in the time you are in right now.

If you are in a season of parenting, working part or full-time, good on you! Give yourself permission to do what you need to do, in order to set yourself up for a win.

If you are a career person and need to get a cleaner, or other worker, to help you achieve your best life, give yourself permission to do that.

Whatever you need to do to achieve your best life, (as long as it's not hurting anyone) give yourself permission to be your best self and achieve greatness, or even permission to get through the day, one moment at a time.

On the next page, I have written a permission note, for you. You can change it and make it your own. I want you to believe and live out of the permission that is yours!

I have permission to live my best life, now!
I live a life fearless and when I do feel fear arise, I choose to use that fear to motivate me, to step out beyond myself and look fear in the eye and say, 'Look out, I'm coming through.'

I am thankful for my past and the challenges that have made me into the person I am today.
I choose to live in the moment and not let my past determine my future.
I give myself permission to let go of anything holding me back and I drop the walls I have put up around myself to protect me, for they no longer serve a purpose for where I'm going.

I have permission to enjoy every moment of my life, both the good moments and to use the not so good times to learn and grow into being an even better version of myself.

I have full permission to live under the power of the Holy Spirit and to not live under any person's control.

I have permission to be all God's called me to be and to access my inheritance now!

Say 'Yes'

I love that in the Bible, God chose ordinary people. God called the least likely of people, and did extraordinary things through them. The way God has done things from the beginning of time, is so countercultural to our world.

Time and time again, people were given opportunities, to say 'yes' and can you imagine, if they didn't. Today we could be living in a much different world than the one we live in.

Moses leading the Israelites out of Egypt, David taking on Goliath, Esther, Joseph and of course, as mentioned earlier the beautiful, courageous Mary, the mother of Jesus.

They said 'yes' to the unknown, the uncomfortable and said 'yes', in spite of their fear.

God asked for their 'yes' and they had a choice in what their response would be. They could have let what people thought of them or their heritage or their past, determine their answer to the question. But they all chose to say 'yes.' They did it, not knowing the future and they did it afraid. There are so many opportunities waiting on the other side of your 'yes.'

Declare

The words we speak have power. In Proverbs it says, *'Death and life are in the power of the tongue, and those who love it will eat its fruits.'* (Proverbs 18.21 ESV)

Do you speak life over yourself, your circumstances, your family and in the areas you are believing for breakthrough?

I have seen so much breakthrough, through declaring and speaking

God's word over a situation. We live in a day and age where it seems popular to flippantly speak words that are less than positive and life-giving over ourselves and one another?

'Hey Nerd,' 'Hey Ugly,' 'Hey Weirdo' seem to be terms of endearment, people say to their family members and other people they like. To be honest I just don't understand that. Even if this is a way people speak, it doesn't mean we need to adopt this cultural trend as our own. Our words have power, to have life or death or curse.

There are so many people suffering with different social and mental anxieties. I wonder what would happen if we made a conscious effort to be aware of what comes out of our mouths. What if, instead of calling each other derogatory names, we spoke life-giving words over one another?

Take an inventory of what comes out of your mouth. Even if for a day, take a language stocktake on what you say over yourself, your family, loved ones and other people.

Romans 4 says, *'as it is written, "I have made you a father of many nations" in the presence of Him whom he believed - God, who gives life to the dead and calls those things which do not exist as though they did.'* (Romans 4.17 ESV)

Declaration can be a standard we set in our lives. If we are believing for a miracle, why do we continue to speak about what we see in the natural? We can get stuck focusing on the lack, pain, loss and use our words to reinforce these circumstances. I wonder what would happen if we creatively started speaking into being what we are hoping and believing for?

Whatever you are believing for, whether it be salvation for a family member, healing for yourself or a loved one, a miracle in your finances, or anything else, I encourage you to declare life, and speak whatever you are believing for, into existence.

Maybe, there's things that you feel are dead in your life. Dreams of working in a particular job or believing for your significant other or for a prodigal to return to the Lord, or restoration in a relationship. God speaks life over dry bones where there is no hope, to live and breathe by the Spirit of God.

God reminds us in Ezekiel 37 to speak or prophesy over dead things. Where there's no hope or areas of our lives that look dead, we can speak God's perspective and see hope and life return, simply by our declaration.

Wow! What in your life might need a word that brings it to life? Is it a family member that feels so far removed and reconciliation seems impossible? A health need in your life that you have been believing for breakthrough for a long time? An addiction you have been battling with that no one else knows of, that you feel so ashamed about? A dream you allowed to fall by the wayside, that needs to be revived? A feeling of despair, disappointment, or shame that has got a grip of your soul?

Whatever it is, I want you to take time at the end of this chapter, or go there now if you like, and get before God. Lift those things up to Him. Once you've done that, I want you to ask God for his perspective on those things. Then listen. You might like to write down God's perspective. This might come in pictures or a song, you may like to draw or create. A scripture might pop into your mind, or a feeling of peace might settle on your soul. Use this listening time to form your very specific and intentional declaration. Even if it is a single word, or a feeling without words, this is your key to begin forming your life-giving words to speak over whatever you are believing God for.

> God's perspective always speaks life
> into every circumstance.

Whether you've been believing for a breakthrough for five days or fifty-five years, it is never too late to speak life over those dead bones.

Years ago, I had an issue with a work colleague. I couldn't pinpoint what it was but knew there was an underlying issue. Sometimes there are things that you can confront or talk about, and sometimes prayer is the best way to go. I have learnt this the hard way. With this situation, nothing was done or said that would warrant going to the person. I have learnt to ask for wisdom from Heaven in these situations, on whether to go to the person, or whether to pray and storm Heaven.

In this case, I stormed Heaven. Every morning I would declare life over this person. I would thank God for them and the strength they brought to the work place. For their gifts and talents (I spoke them out) and then declared blessing for them and for their family.

It wasn't long after I started doing this, I noticed a distinct change in this person's interaction with me. I had tried every effort in my own strength, and it took declaring life, declaring what I couldn't see yet, into reality.

Sometimes it is hard to find the good in people who we have issues with. If we choose to look through Jesus' lens, there is always something we can be thankful for in the person.

What would it look like, if when we thought about the person bothering us, we listed their good points? Even when speaking to them we could choose to give them encouragement on a skill or attribute where they excel? I guarantee this simple practice will have astounding effects for them, and for your relationship with them.

A few years ago, I started writing, declarations I read over myself for the coming year. They are made up of different quotes, verses, prophetic words and revelations previously given to me. Declaring these words of life, every morning, over myself, has had life-changing results. I have shared this exercise with others, and seen breakthrough in many lives.

I will share one of my declarations over the last couple of years with you:

I was born on purpose, for purpose, to bring influence and to change culture. I am confident, fearless and free. Free to be me and to liberate those around me.

I have a banner of freedom over me and I walk in wholeness. I walk in love. I choose to access all God has for me.

I am a daughter of The Most High God and I was born to make manifest the glory of God!

I am content in every season!

I am a light in the world, the head and not the tail, a woman who radiates Jesus to everyone I meet, to reveal the freedom, hope, peace and joy I have in Him now!

The same power that raised Christ from the dead, lives in me.

I have the mind of Christ, I speak the truth in love. I am His hands, feet and mouth to everyone I meet.

I speak words of life, over myself and others.

I choose to walk in joy and in the authority and power I have been given by my Father.

I choose intimacy with my Father, over any love of the world. I choose to lean into Him, during every season of my life.

I am called, chosen, beloved, healed, whole, spirit, soul and body, anointed, highly favoured, blessed and loved beyond measure.

I am a woman of worth, far above rubies. I am worthy of love. I am enough!

I stand in alignment with who Christ says I am.

I am a good steward with my time, energy, health and resource, and Heaven is opened over me, storehouses unlocked, provision and God's resources flow.

I am convinced that every detail of my life is continually woven together, to fit into Christ's perfect plan, of bringing good into my life, for I am His lover, who He has called to fulfil His designed purpose, to share the likeness of Jesus.

I am an investor into my breath-taking future.

I have a global voice.

I am righteous, redeemed and free, to walk in ALL my Father has for me, to bring glory to His name!

I have seen many miracles come to pass from declaring these words over my life. Things that seemed so out of reach, promises that God had given to me but I hadn't seen any traction on.

For one entire year I read these life-giving words over myself. Every morning I would intentionally agree in my spirit with each of these words.

I encourage you too, to find scriptures, revisit previous prophetic words and write your own declaration. Speaking your personal declaration over yourself daily, will bring transformation to your life.

As I have mentioned earlier, I have known from a very young age that God has called me for something bigger than myself. He challenged me to declare what He has shown me is in my future. Just like I'm challenging you. So, I added 'I have a global voice', to my daily declaration.

A few months after the addition, I was asked to meet with my Senior Pastor, Darlene Zschech. She told me she had something she wanted to ask me. I was excited, and realised when I saw her face, that she was excited too. The conversation went something like this. 'I had a dream of starting an online campus and I saw the campus pastor and it was you.' With me sitting there, like a stunned mullet, I was asked to be the online campus pastor.

Almost a year later, from that initial conversation, (and believe me there is a whole God set up and how He prepared me 'for such a time as this' moment) we now broadcast to thousands of people, all over the world, each and every Sunday. I have a global voice!

Declaration! I cannot express how truly important this is.

Again, Jesus is our example of how we should live our lives. Rest assured, Jesus didn't go around putting people down. He spoke the truth, in love, and said things that would set people free. Let's choose today, to speak life over ourselves and over every person who crosses our path. Our journey with Jesus starts with belief and declaration.

'The message is very close at hand; it is on your lips and in your heart.' And that message is the very message about faith that we preach: If you openly declare that Jesus is Lord and believe in your heart that God raised Him from the dead, you will be saved. For it is by believing in your heart that you are made right with God, and it is by openly declaring your faith that you are saved.' (Romans 10.8-10 NLT)

I love that communion with God begins with a declaration and believing in your heart. What we declare says a lot about us. If you want to know what is important to people, listen to what comes out of their mouth.

I can't tell you how many conferences I've been to where I've walked away so motivated and ready to take on the world. Unfortunately, it doesn't take long, to get into the daily grind and demands of life, until that motivation is long gone. I need to encourage myself daily, to do what is in front of me to do, in the trajectory I am on.

Ephesians 3.20 is one of my favourite scriptures. Let's look at it in a few different translations.

'Now to Him who is able to do exceedingly abundantly above all that we ask or think, according to the power that works in us.' (NKJV)

'God can do anything, you know - far more than you could ever imagine or guess or request in your wildest dreams! He does it not by pushing us around but by working within us, His Spirit deeply and gently within us.' (MSG)

'Never doubt God's mighty power to work in you and accomplish all this. He will achieve infinitely more than your greatest request, your most unbelievable dream and exceed your wildest imagination! He will outdo them all, for His miraculous power constantly energises you.' (TPT)

Wow! This is for you, yes you! We can live a life better than our wildest dreams. Just imagine that for a moment! Take a moment now and think about the fullness of what you have just read.

Even if the people around you don't see your bright future, you know that God's mighty plans for you are beyond your wildest imaginations.

When we are in alignment with God's will in our life, we can do abundantly more than others can dream for our life and what even we can imagine. According to dictionary.com abundance is *'present in great quality, more than adequate, over sufficient'*

We have the power and the authority to speak the name of Jesus over every area of our life. Over our health, our family, our employment, our finances, over every sphere of our influence.

It's time to dream big, give ourselves permission and declare our way to greatness.

With God on our side, we can do anything!

> The very area of weakness is going to be your greatest strength.

APP

- What do you need to give yourself permission to do?
- Is there someone in your world you need to pray and declare life over? If so start today.
- Write your own declaration and start declaring it daily over yourself.

Chapter 6
Thankful Heart

'I'm thanking You, God, from a full heart, I'm writing the book on Your wonders. I'm whistling, laughing and jumping for joy; I'm singing Your song, High God.'
(Psalm 9.1,2 MSG)

So many times in my life, I have seen my circumstances change, for the better, due to intentionally having a thankful heart. It has become a daily practise of mine that before I get out of bed and just before I go to sleep at night, to be thankful and say to the Lord what I'm grateful for.

There is scientific evidence from the field of Neuropsychology, to say the practise of gratefulness actually changes chemicals in the brain.

Much like in the previous chapter on declaring life, there have been times when there has been an underlying issue with someone in my world. Something I couldn't quite pinpoint, however, I knew something was there. I have prayed for the particular person and every time, a change happens between myself and them. I can't explain it, however, I'm convinced it's the power of prayer and the practise of gratefulness combined that have definitely influenced the situation.

There is something in every single person, that we can be thankful for. Every person has strengths, because they're created in the image of God, and He is all good!

I love that there are opportunities to pray for people. I will pray every morning and night for particular people. I have seen breakthrough in people's health, finances and seen families reconciled.

Thankfulness, I believe changes the atmosphere. In our everyday lives, there is always something to be thankful for. If we have breath in our lungs, we have something to praise God for.

I live on the coast of New South Wales, Australia and in my opinion, the most beautiful, blessed country in the world. It's also known as the great southland of the Holy Spirit. I often thank God for being born in this generation, to the family I was born into and to have been born in Australia.

The natural beauty, our medical systems, our roads and our services. The Aussie culture, generally speaking, is that when the times are tough, we help one another out.

I remember saying to my mum as a little girl, 'I wish I could wear normal shoes' and she would respond, 'there are people who don't have feet.' I am so grateful to my parents, for bringing me up, to remember that there is always someone worse off than yourself. I learnt to be thankful I had feet that I could walk on. It takes away any room for pity. I cannot stand pity.

That, right there, changes your perspective.

Over one hundred times in the Bible, it speaks of gratefulness.

It is important to RENEW our minds, daily.

How do we develop the language of the Kingdom? We practise.

We can set up new habits and can even change the plasticity in our brains.

We have the power to refocus, renew our minds and create new daily habits.

As I mentioned earlier I wake up and choose to say three things I am thankful for and then again before I go to sleep. This changes my neural pathways and helps me to develop a habit of gratitude. I want to be a woman who is grateful, who can look at the good in every situation and see the gold in every person, whilst remaining authentic.

Both thankfulness and complaining is like a muscle that grows as we use it.

I am committed to intentionally be a woman that is grateful and not to complain. To daily use the language of the Kingdom and not engage with the language of the enemy. If I slip, I will replace the complaining or negative attitude with three things I am grateful for.

I know since doing this, I can feel a spiritual expansion of my heart. There is a physiological reaction in my body. That muscle is growing.

How good would it be if we were deliberate about being grateful every day?

I wonder what would happen if when we interacted with people we could be grateful for who they are and the strengths they have? I think this would unlock gratefulness in others. We could lead with gratefulness and influence others in doing so. It would be infectious.

Have you ever had someone say to you, there's something different about you? We should stand out, as Kingdom men and women, as a people who are grateful.

If we get into negativity, we can rely on the Holy Spirit to prompt us if we are having a negative moment. We can rely on His strength and instead of looking on the circumstance in front of us or the attitude someone is displaying, we can choose to be grateful for something in the circumstance or for the person standing in front of us.

As Christians, we can live above our circumstances.

These are a couple of my favourite scriptures on being thankful.

'Above all, clothe yourselves with love, which binds us all together in perfect harmony. And let the peace that comes from Christ rule in your hearts. For as members of one body you are called to live in peace. And always be thankful. Let the message about Christ, in all its richness, fill your lives. Teach and counsel each other with all the wisdom He gives. Sing psalms and hymns and spiritual songs to God with thankful hearts.' (Colossians 3.14-16 NLT)

'Be thankful in all circumstances, for this is God's will for you who belong to Christ Jesus.' (1 Thessalonians 5.18 NLT)

Do you naturally tend to lean to the positive or negative in life?

I'm sure you've seen it, there are people that no matter what the circumstance or season of life, they always have a smile on their face and a positive outlook on life.

Then there are others, that you see coming and it looks like they've eaten a bag of sour lemons. Sad thing is, this is their 24/7, 365-day look. I can assure you, this does not just appear on the face, this is to do with mindsets and what's going on in their hearts.

Negativity can very slowly creep in and ultimately affect your perspective, your attitude and if it leads to bitterness, can affect your body.

Unresolved negativity can have a negative effect on your mental, spiritual and physical health. Therefore, it's very important to deal with it, as it arises.

I want to be known as a woman who is grateful, positive and while being authentic, can look at the good in every situation and in every person.

Being thankful changes our perspective, from what we don't have, to focusing on what we are blessed with.

> Gratitude is the language of the Kingdom and complaining and negativity are the language of the enemy.

FOCUS

What we focus on grows bigger. Have you ever had something you've been thinking on, become all-consuming? That is because it was first a thought that when focused on, grew and grew, then before you realise, it's all you think about.

This can be in the negative, but it can also be used to redirect ourselves, in a positive way too.

For years now I have had a vision board in my room. I have things on there that I believe God has called me for, things I am passionate about, areas of growth and my heart's desires. Every morning when I wake up, it's the first thing that I see. It's a reminder of the direction I am heading and what I am trying to achieve.

There are sticky notes all over my house. Gentle reminders to focus on who I am and whose I am.

There is so much negativity in the world. It's good to choose to be intentional with what you focus on. What you look at and what you speak over yourself, I believe, is more important than we realise.

A few years ago, I went on a six-week holiday to the United States of America. I have friends over there, so had been to see them and then I was meeting up with a friend from home, to go on an eighteen-day bus tour across the country. I have done these tours before and they are a great way to get around and see a lot of the country in a short amount of time. When my friend arrived in New York, which is where the tour was leaving from, I couldn't wait to show her the sights and if you've ever been there, there is so much to see and do in New York City.

We went all around the city, on the hop-on-hop-off bus. We saw the Statue of Liberty, went to the top of the Empire State Building and we hired bikes and rode around Central Park. It seemed like a wonderful idea at the time. It is something I'd wanted to do for a long time.

We hired the bikes and went over to the park. Central Park would, in my opinion, be the most beautiful park I've ever seen. I love all the architecture and the little themes around. It is HUGE! We started with coffee in the boat house. Watching the row boats was great.

Off we headed on our bike tour around the park. I had planned (as I do) the route we'd take, and all the sights were marked out and I was so happy to be showing my friend all the different places inside this magnificent park. (as this was my third time doing this)

There are lots of places you can only 'walk' your bike, you are not allowed to ride, so in spite of getting the bikes to save our walking, we still had to walk, a lot. We got lost and had to walk up many stairs, carrying our bikes.

We were both exhausted by the end of it. It wasn't quite as dreamy as I had imagined and planned out in my mind. We dropped the bikes off and kept touring the city until after dark, then we went to see a broadway show.

After the show and a full day in the city, my knees were in chronic pain. I hadn't ridden a bike in quite a few years, so thought it may have been after our big day, around the park and lots of walking in this amazing city. On the way back to our hotel, I felt my knee just give way and it felt like something had snapped. It was very painful. I was trying to be tough around my friend, but the tears came streaming out. I was thinking 'oh no, we're leaving in the morning for a tour across America, I need to be okay.' Every step I took was agony.

We got back to the hotel, shortly before midnight, I had a shower and put my feet up and rested. The next morning, we all met in the lobby and joined the rest of the tourists, for our eighteen-day tour.

We headed off nice and early. I was trying to look strong and praying my knee would be healed and this tour would go according to plan.

The days were long, leaving around 7am and returning most nights, to our next destinations hotel around 6pm. It was amazing seeing the beautiful countryside and different states. Most nights I would get back to the hotels and be in excruciating pain.

My friend asked the tour guide what would happen if hypothetically, someone couldn't keep going on the tour, due to health reasons and he told her that they would drop the person (knowing she was asking about me) to the local hospital and they would have to keep going on the tour, as planned.

One morning, my friend got up and asked, 'you ready to go to breakfast?' I explained I was going to spend time with God. This has always been part of my daily practise, but I knew I needed to storm Heaven on this morning.

My heart was filled with fear. I felt fear in a way I hadn't ever felt it before. It gripped my very being. I was thinking (obviously you can tell by now, I am a high thinker) what if they have to keep going and take me to hospital? A lot of other negative thoughts were being magnified the more I thought and dwelt on them.

When she left the room, I put on a song and cried, prayed and stormed Heaven. I declared Jesus over my body, speaking against fear, and declared I am healed and whole. I worshipped until the words became more than a song and my heart was filled with a new perspective and my focus had changed from the pain and fear I had been experiencing, to focusing on who I was and who God was and what He had done for me.

When my friend returned from breakfast she walked in and immediately asked if I was better, as she said I looked different.

Let me be very honest here, my pain had not changed, it was my perspective that had changed.

The rest of the trip was so much better than the first part, simply due to my focus. When I felt pain and fear arise I would be intentional to refocus from the pain to fixing my eyes on Jesus.

When returning home, I went and saw an orthopaedic surgeon and there was significant damage, thought to have been from the bike ride, around that gorgeous park, which explained the excruciating pain. This lesson, on focus, I had learnt on this trip was invaluable.

Lens change

I believe God is calling us to a lens change. Asking us how do we see ourselves? Do we see ourselves as He sees us? Do we realise how Heaven sees us? I think if we did, we would live our lives very differently, it would change our whole posture.

Recently I heard someone share, that a man was in a Christian meeting and he saw this bright, fiery being. He asked the Lord if it was an angel. God replied 'no.' Then the man asked if it was the Holy Spirit, to which God replied 'no.' 'Well, who is it?' the man asked. God replied to the man 'that is you and that is how you are seen in the spirit realm.' Wow! Selah right there.

Imagine, just for a moment, if we viewed ourselves as Heaven recognised us. What would that look like? Maybe spend some time asking God, what you look like. This isn't just airy-fairy words here; this is us desiring God's perspective of ourselves.

Since hearing this story, I have been asking. I pray that as I journey this, it will be a revelation to my heart and soul and therefore I will walk in the natural, with the confidence of Heaven.

When Joshua and Caleb went out to scout the Promised Land, their lens was very different to the others who went out and therefore their report was very different.

The others came back seeing powerful giants in the land and said, *'Next to them we felt like grasshoppers and that's what they thought too.'* (Numbers 13.33 NLT)

> How we see, affects the way we view ourselves, others and situations we are facing.

The other ten spies who went out had a different lens, that saw the giants and saw the challenges they would face. But Caleb and Joshua, while they saw the giants, they had a lens that saw opportunities and could see BEYOND the giants in front of them.

This is important in life, to look beyond what we see in the natural and have an eternal perspective.

Imagine, if you looked beyond your giant and saw yourself. What would you see? A confident, courageous person, who had just overcome the giants of the land? If only we could look beyond the giants, we would position ourselves to approach the land in a different way. We would have the plan and know the outcome.

Years ago, I took my son to see the new Karate Kid movie. I wondered how the new one might compare with the old 1980s one.

Towards the end of the movie, young Dre was in the tournament fight and it looked like he was being defeated. He was so small, compared to his opponent and it looked like he would be defeated and out of the competition. I felt sad for him.

Then it dawned on me, hold on, I know the end of the movie, because I've seen the original. Of course, he wins. My sadness immediately turned to joy, enjoying the rest of the movie.

Mr Han, his trainer and friend, had trained him well and Dre was ready for whatever would come his way. This is the same way, when looking at the giants in the land that we might be facing. We've done the training, so with God by our side, we can face any giant.

Years ago, after I left that toxic relationship, I lived in fear for a long time. That person was the only person I had ever been afraid of.

Growing up, I was the tough one. If my friends and I heard a noise, it would be me who went out to investigate, as they were hiding with their heads under the bed. In this toxic relationship, the person was a little more than physically intimidating.

One day I was walking, and God pointed out my shadow. He showed me how big my shadow was, in comparison to the reality of my actual height and size. He showed me that I viewed this person, much bigger than they actually were. Because I would focus on them, fearful of whether they would find me, I was in actual fact, magnifying the issue, making them bigger than they actually were and therefore increasing my fear levels.

What if we took a look at the giants, with a new lens, with a new focus? What if we had the outlook and the courage of Joshua and Caleb?

Imagine if we went into every battle, knowing the battle is already won! Wow, that sure would be a lens change.

'We entered the land you sent us to explore, and it is indeed a bountiful country – a land flowing with milk and honey. Here is the kind of fruit it produces. But the people living there are powerful, and their towns are large and fortified. We even saw giants there, the descendants of Anak! Caleb goes on to say, 'Let's go at once to take the land, we can certainly conquer it.' (Numbers 13.27,28, 30 NLT)

They saw the land beyond the giants. They saw themselves beyond the giants.

Are you focusing on the giants of your past?

> Your past does not determine your future – unless you let it!

At the time of writing this, I'm in my mid-forties and I look back on my life, to what God has done in me and I am overwhelmed at His faithfulness, patience with me and His goodness at turning all the rubbish into good.

I could choose to allow what happened around my birth, or abuse in my toxic relationship affect the person I am today.

You can allow your circumstances to get on top of you, or you can get on top of them. The choice is yours.

I once heard a story about two brothers who had a father who was an alcoholic. They grew into young men. One son became an alcoholic and had nowhere to live. The other son never touched a drop of alcohol and was a successful, wealthy man. When asked why they made those life decisions they both answered because of their father.

You can choose to let your past define you. There are scars that we carry, that may be part of who we are, however, we do not have to let them define us to the point of holding us back or stepping into all that is ahead for us.

I know I have scars from my past, physical and emotional. I do hope that I have come through the fire not smelling of smoke, so to speak.

Without my past, I would not be the person I am today. As gruelling as some seasons have been, I would not change my life, one bit. Even the less than great choices I have made, I have seen God turn all of these around for His glory.

'And we know that all things work together for good to those who love God, to those called according to His purpose.' (Romans 8.28 NKJV)

> Our past can be a stumbling block or a stepping stone – the choice is yours!

Do I view myself with the lens of God? Do I view myself as God sees me, or with tainted, stained glasses?

How do I see others? With the lens of God, or with my perspective and judgmental view?
Great questions to ask ourselves, regularly.

When I was seven, I was attending a small Christian school that was run through our church. The twenty or so that attended all went to our church, so it was like one big, happy family. My best friend went there. Our mothers were pregnant at the same time and we grew up very close.

Our school was learning a song to sing in front of our families. It was called 'If I were a butterfly.' My best friend was chosen to be the butterfly. Of course she was. She was blonde and beautiful. Even back then when we were little seven-year olds, I could see she was stunning.

I was chosen to be the fuzzy, wuzzy bear. Those that know me, know my hair is a sore point. I say it's like Mufasa from the Lion King. Big and frizzy. (thankful for hair straigtheners)

I remember wanting to be the beautiful butterfly and feeling very disappointed when I was told I would be the fuzzy wuzzy bear. After all a bear is a boy animal, right?

My lens, even at the age of seven, was that I was not beautiful. My lens was fractured and therefore affected the way I saw myself and therefore my belief system.

Imagine how our life would be if we magnified God and focused our attention onto Him, more than the mountain we're facing, more than the worry or anxiety we are feeling? As simple as this sounds, this is a game changer. We can choose to make God bigger than the mountain.

There are many scriptures on 'Magnifying the Lord.'

'And Mary said: 'My soul magnifies the Lord.' (Luke 1.46 NKJV)

'I will praise the name of God with a song, and I will magnify Him with thanksgiving.' (Psalm 69.30 NKJV)

Let's be mindful, next time we are feeling overwhelmed due to the mountain we're facing, when our soul is getting loud, that we intentionally magnify the Lord, instead of magnifying our problem. Selah!

I want to live with the lens of Christ. For Jesus's eyes to be my mirror. Imagine if every morning I woke up and said, 'Jesus, give me Your eyes to see myself, the way You see me this morning.' That would most certainly set my day up right. Then when I go out and order my coffee, or see my co-worker, what if I said, 'Jesus give me eyes to see this person how You see them?' Wow! My whole day would be different when I intentionally choose to live this way and how I view the lives of those I come across.

Philippians 2.5 (MSG) says *'Think of yourselves the way Christ Jesus thought of Himself.'* The Passion Translation says, *'Let His mindset become your motivation.'*

These are big verses. We can only do this with the help of Holy Spirit and personal practises, to daily ask God to give us eyes to see, with a new lens, with His lens.

Eternal Perspective

'While we look not at the things which are seen, but at the things which are not seen; for the things which are seen are temporal, but the things which are not seen are eternal.' (2 Corinthians 4.18 NKJV)

When we focus on our mountain or the situation we are facing, it becomes larger, as we are magnifying it. When we put our trust in God, we have given Him the mountain or situation to move in a way only He can.

We all have things that we are believing to come to pass. I can assure you that the mountain we are looking at, even though it might be the only thing we see, God is moving in the unseen. He never sleeps nor slumbers, He is on the job! Our mountain, situation or season is only temporary, but what God is doing, is going to have eternal ramifications. The heart of the family member you're believing God to bring back to Him, the financial situation you're believing He will turn around, the sickness you're standing on His word to do a miracle in. He's moving in the unseen.

So, what would having an eternal perspective look like?

Looking beyond the temporary. Seeing beyond the attitude of the person in front of you and asking God to show you their heart.

Looking beyond the obstacles, the negative things you see and seeing the richness in the person or situation before you.

Years ago, I used to take a young woman to church. She was a beautiful girl, with a background of tragedy and trauma like you wouldn't believe. Her children had been removed and to feed her addictions, she was engaging in activities that did not bring value to her and were unsafe.

I would look at this girl and my heart would break. I wondered why, when my church family looked at her, their hearts didn't break too.

Now this is going back many years ago, before I learnt to bridle my tongue and I used to get myself in trouble for my abrupt ways of dealing with the injustice I saw. I would like to think it was righteous anger but I do know there was a lot of my flesh in there too.

This day she walked into church and she looked around, feeling unworthy. She said to me, as she looked and pointed to a lady in church, who, in her mind, appeared to have it all together, (as we can get good at putting on our Sunday best) 'How will I ever be like her?' If ever my heart broke, it was right there in that moment. My friend was comparing what she felt was an unworthy life, to this other lady's life, who I knew equally felt unworthy but had just learnt to wear a mask to disguise that unworthiness. I explained to her, with tears in my eyes, that she is worthy and proceeded to tell her who she was in Christ, however I'm not sure she believed it, at the time.

Today, this beautiful lady is a great friend of mine. She has overcome many obstacles and challenges and is an empowered, Christian woman in her community, helping others.

We need to be aware of how we treat people. The enemy tries to use this lie often. If he can make us feel unworthy, he can keep us from fulfilling God's plan and purpose for our lives. When we feel unworthy, we don't feel like we can do what God's called us to do. The enemy loves to distract us from the truth of who we are in Christ.

I do not want to get to Heaven, and for God to say, 'I gave you all of these tools, but you only used a small part of what I gave you access to, due to your limited vision or perspective.'

I want to have an eternal perspective. His perspective. I want to see Heaven come to Earth. I won't get too far ahead of myself, though as I'll discuss this a little later.

Before I moved back home, ten years ago now, after a very long ten years of healing, living away from family, my pastors prayed and prophesied over me on my last Sunday at church. The beautiful couple both gave me a word, and both were spot on. One went something like this: Kylie you are like a beautiful Persian rug. It's beautiful to those who see you. You, however, see the back of the rug, where there are little knots and ends tied-up. Jesus sees you as the other side. Beautiful, whole and complete.

We can so often look at our faults, our scars and not look at the beauty in ourselves and how far we have come.

Something we don't do a lot of today is to imagine. Our imagination is a gift God has given to us. It is good to take time aside to imagine.

'For we walk by faith, not by sight.' (2 Corinthians 5.7 NKJV) I love how the Message says it, *'It's what we trust in but don't yet see that keeps us going.'*

'Set your mind on things above, not on things that are on Earth.' (Colossians 3.2 NKJV)

'Set your gaze on the path before you with fixed purpose, looking straight ahead, ignore life's distractions.' (Proverbs 4.25 TPT)

APP

- Can you see yourself beyond the giants? What do you look like?
- How do you see yourself?
- What can you do to replace your lens for God's lens today?

Chapter 7

Forgiveness

'Forgiveness is for yourself because it frees you. It lets you out of that prison you put yourself in.'
(Louise Hay)

Understanding the power of forgiveness is key for all of us. Whether you are a believer or not, there is power in forgiveness.

Forgiving someone, does not make what they did to you okay. It does not mean that you agree or give the person permission to keep doing what they did that was wrong to you. Forgiving is more about you than them. I forgive because I was forgiven, by the One who knew no sin.

From a young age, I have understood the power of this intentional choice to forgive. There have been varying degrees on how I've outworked forgiveness, but I have made it part of my life, to forgive quickly.

Before I go to sleep at night I reflect upon my day and forgive and let go of anything I do not want to take into my next day. In the many support groups I have been a part of, I have learnt and taught different practical ways to do this.

One way is to write a letter to the person who did you wrong. Say exactly what you need to say. Usually, the letter isn't to send to the person (especially if it's not safe to do so) it's more for you to be able to get everything out and all those emotions articulated on paper. Then when you've sat in that for a while, and you feel ready, rip up that letter and release those feelings of anger, shame, worthlessness and unforgiveness.

I have used a similar method by asking those who are in a support group to write on a balloon and then popping it, when they feel ready.

Who do you think was the hardest person in my life to forgive? Most would assume the person with whom I had a toxic relationship. The person I found hardest to forgive, way more than any other person, was myself.

Entering into that relationship in my life, was something I did when I felt God say not to. Very clearly when I asked God about this relationship, I heard Him say to my heart 'no, not now.' Three simple yet powerful words.

I chose to twist those words and help God in the process of making this relationship go a little faster, according to my time frame. As we know God's timing is often a tad longer than ours.

When God said those three little words 'no, not now,' I thought ok, not now, but that means 'yes, one day.' Hmmm, how about if I helped this person work through their problems, I'd be helping it come along a little faster and we will live happily ever after.

Well, it didn't work out quite like that. In fact, there were consequences, that didn't just affect me at the time but others around me. Today those affected and myself are still living with the consequences of my disobedience. I know that I am forgiven for not heeding God's wisdom at that time. The issue was harder when I had to forgive myself for not listening.

Forgiveness, has been a process. Someone pointed out to me, I needed to forgive myself – to let go of the guilt and shame I was carrying. 'I should have known better.' 'How did I not see what this person was like?'

Have you ever asked yourself questions like that?

> When you let go of unforgiveness and other things that weigh you down, it releases freedom in your life.

That freedom can't be bought, it is a feeling like no other.

The other person I had to forgive, was the one with whom I had a toxic relationship. Although I said I had a revelation of forgiveness from a young age, the practical application of forgiveness was interesting to say the least.

After exiting the relationship, I forgave. As the abuse and threats came in after I had left, I continued to forgive. As I mentioned previously, forgiving does not, I repeat, does not, give a person the right to abuse you. It does not make what they did okay.

Growing up in the Christian lifestyle, I think now, in my older and hopefully wiser years, that some of the teachings around forgiveness I heard when I was young, may not necessarily be correct for me today.

I remember a little acronym I learned when I was younger; JOY. Jesus first, Yourself last and Others in between. I tend to have a different view on that now.

Now, don't get me wrong, do we show kindness to people? Yes, of course we do. However, if you are in any form of abusive relationship, you can very much be empowered to close the door to that. No one on this Earth, deserves to be abused in any way.
I know that this is a delicate subject and I want you to know this is a safe place and I am never condoning any form of exploitation or

injustice to you or anyone. I remember in the beginning, after leaving the toxic person, as things would arise, often daily, I would make the choice to forgive.

I remember saying to God, 'I choose to forgive, but I don't feel like forgiving.' I was like that for a long time. I would repeat this to God, every time I would choose to forgive. It seemed like a monotonous occurrence sometimes.

It went to a whole other level when they didn't just hurt me, they hurt someone I loved. That's when something rises up within you, that you just can't seem to put into words.

I was driving to Sydney one day to see a friend. It's a ninety-minute trip, down the freeway. I love road trips, short and long. When I'm on my own, I love having that extended time with God.

I wasn't too far into the trip and God tugged on my heart around those words I said to Him for years about forgiving this person. 'I choose to forgive, but I don't feel like forgiving.' Ever so gently, He encouraged me to come higher, to let go, and give the burden of that weight to Him.

> We are not designed to carry burdens, such as the heaviness of unforgiveness.

Matthew 11.28 says, *'Come to Me, all you who labour and are heavy laden, and I will give you rest.'* It goes on to say, *'Take My yoke upon you and learn from Me, for I am gentle and lowly in heart, and you will find rest for your souls. For My yoke is easy and My burden is light.'* (Matthew 11.28-30 NKJV)

I wanted to experience that rest for my soul. I could no longer carry around the heaviness of the unjust acts that had been carried out, and that I was carrying. That day I experienced such an emotional release, that I cannot put into words.

I drove up the freeway and spoke out exactly how I felt to each of the people that I needed to forgive, (to do with that person) and I was very emotional in doing so.

If there was a car driving next to me at that time and they saw me, it would have been a show. A woman crying, yelling (not that they would have heard, but could have guessed by hand gestures and the emotional look on my face) as if talking to someone, when I was the only one in the car.

You know though, Holy Spirit was in that car and did what only He can, and held me as the emotions spilled forth in jumbled disarray. The pain, the hurt, the injustice whilst being expressed through my words, was simultaneously washed from my soul as I surrendered.

When the emotions had subsided, I was gifted with the feeling of peace, of calmness and freedom flowing through me. As it says in Matthew, that day I found rest for my soul.

There's a quote from beautiful Marianne Williamson that says, *'Unforgiveness is like drinking poison yourself and waiting for the other person to die.'* That sums it up really well.

The Bible is very clear around forgiveness. Jesus says, *'For if you forgive men their trespasses, your Heavenly Father will also forgive you. But if you do not forgive men their trespasses, neither will your Father forgive your trespasses.'* (Matthew 6.14,15 NKJV)

That is a very clear and direct statement Jesus is saying here. Now lovely one, please hear me when I say, and understand, no one has the right to abuse you, in any way. In getting the forgiveness point across, in no way am I saying what may have happened in your past is okay.

Please hear my heart on this, it is to bring is to bring you healing and freedom, in a way you've only dreamed of.

Forgiveness is key!

> God does not ask us to do anything He will not give us the strength and grace to do.

BOUNDARIES

Boundaries are very important, and I believe are designed by God. In the garden of Eden, God spoke to Adam and Eve and gave them boundaries on what they could and could not eat, all for their good.

Some people do not like when we put boundaries in our life. In fact, it will trigger them, just saying the word 'boundary.'

In Henry Cloud and John Townsend's book, Boundaries: When to Say Yes, How to Say No, to Take Control of Your Life, they say *'Boundaries define us. They define what is me and what is not me. A boundary shows me where I end and someone else begins, leading me to a sense of ownership. Knowing what I am to own and take responsibility for gives me freedom. Taking responsibility for my life opens up many different options. Boundaries help us keep the good in and the bad out. Setting boundaries inevitably involves taking responsibility for your choices. You are the one who makes them. You are the one who must live with their consequences. And you are the one who may be keeping yourself from making the choices you could be happy with. We must own our own thoughts and clarify distorted thinking.'*

I have found the older I get the more I look for the 'why' behind why I do things.

Sometimes, I have wondered if we think that as a Christian, we need to allow people to treat us however they like, to allow them to mistreat and even abuse us and go around that same cycle.

No! No! No! I can tell you, that is a misconception I lived by. You do not have to be mistreated by anyone. As I have said previously, you cannot control what others do, however, you can choose your response to what they do.

I look at Jesus's life when He walked the earth. He was not a push over. He was very intentional with who He spent His time, whilst loving everyone, He didn't put up with nonsense.

There are so many instances of Jesus challenging the Pharisees. Jesus didn't spend a lot of time in their presence hanging out. Putting boundaries in your life is not always easy.

If you are in relationship, whether with a partner, parent, friend, work boss or colleague that is less than healthy, I would encourage you to get the book 'Boundaries' by Henry Cloud and John Townsend. I have read this book numerous times and referred many people to this book, who have had transformational results.

In my four decades of life, I have only had to disassociate with two people. Sometimes boundaries just aren't enough, they need to get out of your life and that might mean you making some tough choices to get to that point, but believe me it is worth it.

Answer the following question:

<u>After you've spent time with a person do you feel:</u>

deflated	loved	secure
safe	heard	accepted
not enough	controlled	put down

Do they refuse to admit they are wrong and blame you for any issues you are having? Whether you are a Christian or not, I can tell you that relationships should be healthy.

You are a person of worth. You were designed by a Creator who modelled healthy boundaries, and we can be encouraged to live the same in all our relationships.

I am so blessed by the friendships I have in my world. They at times challenge me and bring a word of correction, if needed, with their motive always being from love and wanting me to be the best me I can be.

APP

- Do you feel you're carrying the weight of unforgiveness?
- Spend some time in God's presence and ask Holy Spirit to shine the light on any area of unforgiveness you need to take action on.
- Write a letter or set a boundary in an area that has been highlighted in this chapter.

Chapter 8
Kingdom

'But seek first the Kingdom of God and His righteousness, and all these things will be added to you.'
(Matthew 6.33 ESV)

At the time of writing this chapter, we are in a season, that I never thought I would witness, in my lifetime. COVID-19 is a pandemic that has ultimately affected not only our nation but the entire world.

When it broke out, the panic and fear I heard and saw around me, fuelled by constant media attention and news, was like something I'd never seen or heard before. People lost their jobs, couldn't see loved ones, were isolated, and life changed as we knew it. We needed to find a new normal.

When I was at work one day, early on when the restrictions were first being introduced, my boss said we needed to work from home and I burst into tears.

All these thoughts and reminders that I was on my own, lived on my own and isolated, rose up within me. Fear gripped my heart. I went home that day wondering what does this 'new normal' look like and will it be here for long? A question I'd say every person on the planet asked themselves that week.

I went home and spent time in God's presence, seeking His face.

I had got caught up in the culture and panic of what was going on around me, which is easy and can often be a default setting. As I was still before my beautiful God, I was reminded, I do not need to fear, I am in this world, not of this world. I am a citizen of Heaven.

Please hear my heart on this, I understand this is a different experience for every person and I'm not undermining going through the wave of emotions in response to what is going on in the current climate of a global pandemic.

It is important to notice our emotions, name them and seek Heaven's perspective on how to process them. This is a healthy way to work with our emotions rather than be controlled by them.

In that moment, in His presence I was reminded, in all this panic and chaos, He is still on the throne, the Kingdom of God has not shaken and fallen around me, I am safe and secure in Him. It put things into perspective, and I felt His perfect peace fill my heart and mind, like only He can do.

The Kingdom of Heaven is very different to the kingdom of the world in which we live, here and now. I wonder ... does it have to be? ...

Matthew 6.10 (NIV) says, *'Your Kingdom come, Your will be done, on Earth as it is in Heaven.'*

I believe we don't need to wait to get to Heaven to access the Kingdom of God. We can walk and live in that here and now.

Just imagine, for a moment, what 'Heaven on Earth' looks like for you. To walk and live in the culture of Heaven, here and now. That blows my mind, but it's so accessible now.

I can walk, in perfect peace, knowing that God's got it, everything that is consuming my mind, my worries and cares. I don't believe worry is even a word in Heaven. So why should it be here and now? If I'm worrying, I'm relying and trusting in my own abilities and strength to get me out of a situation.

The Kingdom of God or Kingdom of Heaven is mentioned over one hundred and sixty times in the Bible. If we are kingdom people what does that look like living in a world that seems so far away from Heaven's kingdom principles?

When you come into relationship with Jesus, you are a new creation, born again into the Kingdom of God. I am a citizen of Heaven, living on Earth, as a kingdom daughter.

> Kingdom is within you! It's part of your divine heritage.

I would describe myself as a 'kingdom woman,' meaning I live on Earth, but I choose to experience life through a kingdom lens, a kingdom mindset and for my language to have kingdom expression.

I remember having a revelation moment whilst imagining Heaven one day. I was sitting in the sun, looking up at the clouds. I have always loved God's creation, the sky, the clouds, moon and stars, the magnificent sunsets, displaying His majesty. It does something for my soul.

My body was in pain and I was thinking of what it would be like to be in Heaven with no pain, with my new glorified body in perfect alignment. My, how I've dreamed of that, so many times. The words 'on Earth, as in Heaven' came to my heart.

As a daughter of the Most High, I have access to the Kingdom of God, here and now on Earth. Every day I declare over my body healing and wholeness.

Hebrews 4.16 (NLT) says, *'So let us come boldly to the throne of our gracious God. There we will receive His mercy, and we will find grace to help us when we need it most.'*

'The verb translated let us come could be translated to indicate ongoing action; let us continually come. As our compassionate High Priest, Jesus has opened the way for people to enter God's presence boldly, where we can obtain His mercy and grace to help us when we need it most.' (NLT Study Bible)

There are people who can't wait to get to Heaven to access peace and comfort in their lives, after great tragedy and loss. Other people can't wait to get to Heaven to have a rich, full life.

What if you could have an abundant life, a life overflowing, here on Earth, with perfect peace, with strength and endurance, beyond your natural capabilities? Sounds great, right? Well, it's yours. Here and now!

You, as a kingdom son or daughter, have been given access, and all the tools needed to live a kingdom life on Earth. That is a Selah moment right there.

When you think of Heaven, what do you think of?

For me, I believe I'll have a glorified body, no more scars, and pain, physical or emotional. I will no longer get impatient with people. I will walk in perfect peace, because my mind literally will be fixed on Jesus. I can't wait to talk to Jesus, face to face, to glean from Him and stand in His majesty. These thoughts have passed through my mind, numerous times.

So, ... if the Lord's Prayer says, 'on Earth as it is in Heaven,' what if we could have all that here and now?

His supernatural strength and grace are more than enough. We have access to His strength and can align ourselves with grace to access

Heaven here and now on Earth.

CITIZEN

I've had the privilege of travelling to many countries in the world and one thing I've noticed is the different cultures. The culture of Switzerland is very different to the culture in Australia, which contrasts to Scotland, and so on. The world we live in is very diverse and beautifully unique.

A few of my friends have moved to Australia from their homelands (South Africa, France, New Zealand, England and United States of America) and there has been an adjustment made, getting used to the laid-back Aussie culture here in Australia.

To me Australia is home, it's familiar, it's the norm. I have seen people struggle with the new way of life and of course, if separated from loved ones, there is an additional pull at the heart that takes time to process.

When you enter a country, you need to abide by the laws of the country you have entered. It is a whole other level if you become a citizen of that country.

When you become a permanent resident of a country, you take on their culture. It becomes part of you. When you are a citizen of a country, you don't need a visa any longer. You live there, not just visit. There is a King or Queen, President or Prime Minister over each country, and they help determine the culture of that country.

This process is similar when you are 'born again' into Christ. You are no longer your old self; you are in Christ. You have access to all that He has given you.

As an Australian citizen I have access to all that Australia has to offer.

I can travel within the boundaries, I can access health care and other resources that our beautiful country has to offer. I have protection from being exiled out of the country. Being born into this great country of ours, is a continued area of gratitude in my life. Even those that weren't born here and become an Australian citizen, still reap all the benefits, if they become a citizen of Australia.

Now as a daughter of the Most High, I am actually a citizen of Heaven, living here on Earth. You also are a carrier of kingdom culture, here and now. You have the influence and authority to bring Heaven to Earth.

Travelling to other countries, you see cultures are different and one thing that I found a barrier, particularly on my first trip to Paris, was the language.

A moment I will never forget, was with my friend in Paris. It was my first overseas trip and I was so excited. While in France, I wanted to try frog legs. I love to immerse myself in the culture and culinary delights. We decided we would go and have dinner and try this French delicacy. I was excited! We walked down to the lobby of the hotel and tried to ask the lady where we could find a restaurant that had frog legs. I assumed most restaurants had them, in Paris.

The beautiful French lady at reception had been such a help to us during our stay. Her English was very limited, and she had a French/English book to help with anything she needed to interpret. Well this day she needed that book.

Somehow, there was a definite language barrier with me trying to get my question 'Where can we eat frog legs?' The lady looked very puzzled, so I had turned my question into charades, to help get my question answered. I put two fingers up and said 'two words, first word frog' and put my hands like a frog and started making the noise of a frog. My friend was looking at me and I'm sure thinking 'I do not know this girl.' Then it came to the second word, holding two fingers up, I slapped my leg. After some time and that book helping too, between giggles and embarrassment, I was understood and we found ourselves in a, would you believe it, Chinese restaurant, in Paris, eating frog legs. It would be accurate to say that in a foreign country the language difference can be challenging to say the least. Similarly, the language of Heaven is very different to the language of the world.

We, being citizens of Heaven, have the benefit of being able to be bilingual, but our first language should be that of Heaven. The language of Heaven is love, hope, kindness and gratitude.

You will not find negativity in Heaven. There are no problems, only possibilities and the tools and grace on how to position ourselves to access them.

Imagine the unspeakable joy, coming from deep wells within. That is what we can walk in now.

Recently our pastor, Mark Zschech, preached a great message and he said that in the Kingdom, it's upside down to here. Here, it's Me but in Heaven, it's We. The M and the W are upside down, as are a lot of other things. It's upside down to the world's way of thinking, but according to kingdom perspective it is the right way up.

What would it look like for you to bring Heaven to Earth? As a daughter or son and citizen of Heaven you have the jurisdiction to do that.

New Man

On Earth, as Christians, we tend to focus on the old man. We know the scripture 2 Corinthians 5.17 *'Now, if anyone is enfolded into Christ, he has become an entirely new person. All that is related to the old order has vanished. Behold, everything is fresh and new.'* (TPT) Other translations say that the old life is gone (NLT) or passed away. (NKJV)

Why are we trying to revive something that is dead? As citizens of Heaven we live from the new man. The new man or new nature is dead to the things that used to fulfil us and we are alive to newness of our life in Christ. If we sin, it's not because sin is part of our new nature. However, old habits can come to the surface from time to time.

As we understand this in a deeper and revelatory way, we will come to realise we are unlearning our old nature and beginning to walk with this new Christ nature.

If something isn't in Christ, we don't want it. We want to choose to live from that life of abundance, the life of fullness in Him.

One of the best books I have ever read is from an amazing kingdom man, Mark Greenwood. I had the privilege of meeting Mark and his amazingly stunning wife, Christine. This is a couple who have had true revelation of being kingdom citizens.

Mark's book 'Awake to Righteousness' is a must for all kingdom people. Mark writes *'In Christ, we inherit God's righteous nature, not positionally but actually. This also affects our entire being. This becomes experiential in our lives as we engage in intimacy with God, understanding and faithful obedience to the truth. Our independent will must engage with the truth for it to manifest and become our experience.'* (Awake to Righteousness Chapter 5)

As you know, I love justice and everything justice entails. Jesus is justice, it is what He stands for and is one of the many facets of Himself. However, His way of justice and my way often outplay differently.

My way of justice is if things are not fair, or people are not being treated rightly, I have gone in, and no matter what the cost, stood up for those who are being mistreated. Other times I have been known to get angry and people will know about it, when people are being selfish and inconsiderate. How did Jesus demonstrate justice during His time on Earth?

Let's look at some of the stories He told.

We know the scripture about the woman caught in adultery. I love how Jesus responded to the religious people, of the day. I often wonder what He would say now, to us personally, to us as the church and how we treat others. They brought the woman caught in adultery to Jesus and expecting Him to adhere to the culture and laws of the day, she was to be stoned. Jesus, was so calm and self-restrained, even when they were demanding an answer, challenging Him to abide by the rules, to do it the world's way. He simply responded with words that have impacted our generations, over two thousand years later. Jesus said, *'Let him who is without sin among you be the first to throw a stone at her.'* (John 8.7 ESV)

And as we know, they all left, one by one and went on their way and Jesus spoke life and set this woman free.

Justice would say this woman needed to get what she deserved, to adhere to the culture and laws of the day. Jesus brings justice, wrapped in mercy and grace.

Imagine if we got everything we deserved. Jesus gave us mercy and grace, not because we deserve it, but because we are His sons and daughters. Should we not show that same mercy and grace to others? Is that not kingdom culture right there?

Jesus said, *'You have heard that our ancestors were told, 'You must not murder. If you commit murder, you are subject to judgment.' But I say, if you are even angry with someone, you are subject to judgment. If you call someone an idiot, you are in danger of being brought before the court. And if you curse someone you are in danger of the fires of hell.'* (Matthew 5.21-22 NLT)

'You have heard the law that says, 'Love your neighbour' and hate your enemy. But I say, love your enemies! Pray for those who persecute you. In that way, you will be acting as true children of your Father in Heaven.' (Matthew 5.43,44 NLT) It

goes on in verse 48 *'But you are to be perfect, even as your Father in Heaven is perfect.'* *'This word perfect 'means maturity and wholeness in response to Jesus' proclamation of the Kingdom, and complete consecration to God.'* (NLT study notes)

The Kingdom of God has already come, when Jesus came to Earth. When we are born again, we enter a relationship with God, part of our inheritance is that we are citizens of the Kingdom of Heaven.

Jesus spoke the language of Heaven. It wasn't all dramatic and 'Thus saith the Lord.' It was so quiet, yet profoundly heard and received.

Throughout the scriptures, Jesus was the greatest example of being a kingdom person. If you ever want a perfect life model, without doubt, Jesus would be our greatest example. The way Jesus lived is as relevant today as when He walked the Earth.

Kingdom culture doesn't change with the times like the world's culture does. There are fads and crazes and cultural changes with generations, trends and times. The Kingdom of God was established and remains true yesterday, today and forever.

One of the biggest differences I have found is that the world looks on the behaviour or the outside of people, and God looks at the heart.

Some of the differences are:

World culture	Kingdom Culture
our way	God's way
me	God/others
outside behaviours	inner life
transactional relationships	relationships= love
build into me	build into kingdom/eternal
striving	rest
negativity	gratitude
treat others how they deserve	treat others according to their worth
victim	victor
first	last shall be first
least	valued
lead	servant
life is about me, myself & I	refresh others and you too will be refreshed

The kingdom, as a citizen of Heaven, is within you. You carry the very culture and influence of Heaven.

You are a kingdom carrier.

How are you representing the kingdom of God?

I don't know if this is something you know and you are living, or if you are hearing this for the first time. As Dr Phil says, *'We can't change what we don't acknowledge.'* When we know, or are reminded, we are kingdom people, we can change our lens, from world focused glasses to kingdom focused glasses.

'We are seated in heavenly places. Seated at the right hand of the Father.' (Ephesians 2.6 NKJV)

You might be wondering, 'If I'm a citizen of Heaven, living here on Earth, what does that look like?'

I am not influenced or shaken by the culture of what is going on around me. I stand firm on the word of God and knowing that I operate out of a different mindset, a different way of thinking and living. A mindset that may be contrary to the world, however as we, as believers start understanding and standing in the position of kingdom people, we together can bring Heaven to Earth. Wow! Imagine the influence for transformation that would have on those around us and ultimately the world in which we live.

As I said, we are in a world-wide pandemic. Some things have changed, as in the way we did 'normal' life. That is not a bad thing. I can see God's hand in and over this and see so many miracles that have happened. God can use anything and anyone, as we know.

It's not about us sitting back saying 'God, you do it all.' He loves when we take His hand, let Him guide and lead us and we do our part and leave the rest up to Him.

I love that God wants to partner with us.

For example, we are kingdom people and we know that Jehovah Jireh is our provider and that He owns the cattle on a thousand hills. That doesn't mean that as kingdom sons and daughters we sit back and rest and pray all day and believe that God is going to provide for us while we don't have our part to play in this journey of life.

Now please hear my heart on this. First and foremost, we need to run our race and do what God has called us to do. If you are called to full time ministry, do that, partnering with God, if you are called to the market place, do that, partnering with God. If you have limitations where you can't work, this is in no way said in judgement and what and how you live your life is between you and God. What I am saying is for all of us, there is a partnership that happens, where we do our part and God does His.

We do not need to carry the weight of this world. As kingdom people we live from a place of rest. I'm going to go into more detail about rest in the next chapter.

> Kingdom economy is different to the world's economy.

I have seen miracle upon miracle in the areas of finance, in my own life and in the lives of many others. I have seen and heard of people being given money for cars, houses, properties and church buildings.

The world would say to build up our own wealth, to make a nest egg and save. Now all of these things I believe are wise and I do myself. Knowing the economy of the kingdom is knowing that there are storehouses that are open and abundance flows.

Romans says, *'For the Kingdom of God is not a matter of eating and drinking but of righteousness and peace and joy in the Holy Spirit.'* (Romans 14.17 ESV)

Righteousness, peace and joy in the Holy Spirit. Not in my own strength, but partnering with Holy Spirit, my leader, my guide, my everything!

'One day the Pharisees asked Jesus, "When will the Kingdom of God come?" Jesus replied, "The Kingdom of God can't be detected by visible signs. You won't be able to say, 'Here it is!' or 'It's over there!' For the Kingdom of God is already among you." (Luke 7.20,21 NLT)

The Kingdom of Heaven is here now.

A Kingdom has a King. When Jesus left Earth after His resurrection, He left the Holy Spirit here for us. We don't have to do life on our own ever. We have Holy Spirit, every moment of every day to lead and guide us, to fill us with peace, to give us wisdom and supernatural strength.

Everywhere the King is, the Kingdom is. As a citizen of Heaven, everywhere my foot treads I carry and release Heaven's influence. I represent the King in the way I live my life. That can be a scary thought. Am I representing the nature of my King well, in the seen and in the unseen?

THE LORD'S PRAYER

Jesus says "In this manner, therefore, pray: Our Father in Heaven, Hallowed be Your name. Your kingdom come. Your will be done on Earth as it is in Heaven. Give us this day our daily bread. And forgive us our debts, as we forgive our debtors. And do not lead us into temptation, but deliver us from the evil one. For Yours is the kingdom and the power and the glory forever. Amen." (Matthew 6.9-13 NKJV)

This would have to be the most famous prayer that people, who know Christ and even those who don't, have heard. Your kingdom come. Your will be done on Earth as it is in Heaven.

> You, kingdom carrier, have full permission to bring kingdom, to Earth, by being you.

We are seated in heavenly places. Ephesians 2.4-7 (NLT) says *But God is so rich in mercy, and He loved us so much, that even though we were dead because of our sins, He gave us life when He raised Christ from the dead. (It is only by God's grace that you have been saved!) For He raised us from the dead along with Christ and seated us with Him in the heavenly realms because we are united with Christ Jesus. So, God can point to us in all future age's examples of the incredible wealth of His grace and kindness toward us, as shown in all He has done for us who are united with Christ Jesus.'*

'And I will give you the keys of the Kingdom of Heaven. Whatever you forbid on Earth will be forbidden in Heaven, and whatever you permit on Earth will be permitted in Heaven.' (Matthew 16.19 NLT)

If negativity is not in Heaven, I can choose not to accept it or permit it in my life.

Even as writing this chapter, I feel I need to grab a coffee and read and sit in some of these scriptures and revelations.

If we understood that we can align ourselves with Heaven, that we have access to kingdom thinking, economy and the power to bring Heaven to Earth, that right there, is transformational.

I pray that you will take time to pause and to ask God for revelation in the area of being a kingdom son or daughter.

APP

- What has the global pandemic brought up in your life?
- What are you looking forward to in Heaven?
- What practical steps can you take to walk in kingdom culture?

Chapter 9
Freedom

'Now the Lord is the Spirit, and where the Spirit of the Lord is, there is freedom.'
(2 Corinthians 3.17 NIV)

As you've probably picked up throughout the pages of this book, freedom is a word that I love. My most favourite word, after the name above all names, Jesus!

In my forty and some years in this world, I have known what it is like to live in chains holding me back from the fullness and freedom for which Jesus died for me to walk in. There is nothing that compares to that feeling of freedom, once you've experienced it.

I love that we do not have to wait to enter Heaven to experience the liberty that we can walk in now. The freedom that Christ died for us to have.

I remember a defining moment, when I came back to the area that I call home, how different I was to when I left. As a young single mum, I was broken and so deflated with the feeling my life had no hope, and then I was coming home a new woman. As mentioned earlier there were intentional choices made during that ten years of being away, that lead to the freedom that was evident in my life when I came back.

There are so many scriptures in the Bible around freedom. These are my favourites.

'Let me be clear, the Anointed One has set us free – not partially, but completely

and wonderfully free! We must always cherish this truth and stubbornly refuse to go back into the bondage of our past.' (Galatians 5.1 TPT)

The NIV says *'It is for freedom that Christ set us free.'*

'Now the Lord is the Spirit, and where the Spirit of the Lord is, there is freedom.' (ESV) *'Now the Lord is the Spirit, and where the Spirit of the Lord is, there is liberty.' (emancipation from bondage, true freedom) 'And we all, with unveiled face, continually seeing as in a mirror the glory of the Lord, and progressively being transformed into His image from (one degree of) glory to even more glory, which comes from the Lord (who is) the Spirit.'* (AMP) (2 Corinthians 3.17,18)

'Live as people who are free, not using your freedom as a cover-up for evil, but living as servants of God.' (1 Peter 2.16 ESV)

'I will walk with You in complete freedom, for I seek to follow Your every command.' (Psalm 119.45 TPT)

'But now you are free from the power of sin and have become slaves of God. Now you do those things that lead to holiness and result in eternal life. For the wages of sin is death, but the free gift of God is eternal life through Christ Jesus our Lord.' (Romans 6.22, 23 NLT)

Jesus paid such a costly price for our freedom. It cost Jesus His life. Let's never become complacent in the precious, priceless gift that is ours.

After having prayer ministry many years ago with some beautiful people, I remember the elation of leaving that room free, not weighed down, as I was when I walked in the door.

Another time I remember a visiting minister prayed for me, at our church, for one thing and I experienced breakthrough in another area I battled with.

Freedom is ours! Here and now!

Do you walk in the freedom, that is yours to walk in?

There is a story of a man who was passing some elephants, and noticed they were only being contained by a small rope tied to their front leg. There were no chains or cages. The man thought the elephants were strong enough to break free from the rope. The man saw a worker close by and asked why these large elephants just stood there and made no attempt to get away. The worker informed the man that the trainers had trained the elephants, from very young age that the rope around their leg would contain them. As they grew up, they were conditioned to believe they could not escape. The large animal believed the rope could still hold them, so they never tried to break free. These animals could at any time break free from that rope but because they believed they couldn't, they were stuck right where they were. (The Elephant and the Rope)

Every time I hear this story, it reminds me to reflect and ask myself if there is anything holding me back? What held and controlled this great and powerful animal, was conditioning the belief the elephant had from when he was young. We can be carrying around chains, some we may not even be aware of.

Even as you are reading this chapter, I believe the Holy Spirit will speak to your heart and highlight anything that is keeping you from walking in the freedom, Christ died for you to walk in.

> Freedom is already yours! You don't have to wait or save up for it, or until you feel you deserve it. It's been paid for, in full.

How do we receive freedom? We believe.

'But the scriptures declare that we are all prisoners of sin, so we receive God's promise of freedom only by believing in Jesus Christ.' (Galatians 3.22 NLT)
Repeat after me ... 'Freedom is mine!' 'I am free!'

When I have experienced breakthrough in my life, the enemy has tended to come and remind me of what was. I love that we have the authority to stand on what Christ has done, on who we are in Jesus and that we are walking in the fullness of the finished work of the cross. You have been given tools, the authority and position in who you are in Christ, to not allow the enemy to steal anything from you. The thing with the little enemy is that he will try to bring confusion and keep you from knowing who you truly are. I don't like giving the enemy airtime as he has no power over us, unless as I said previously, we allow him.

There are two encounters in the Bible; one in the garden with Eve and the other one in the wilderness with Jesus, where the enemy tried to twist the truth and get them to question who they were. I'm sure we know the stories I'm speaking of. Eve gave into the scheme and was tempted, but Jesus, knowing Who He was, was able to stand against him, by standing on who He was and declaring the word of God. (Genesis 3 and Matthew 4) It is of the utmost importance in our life to know who we are.

> We are in Christ and Christ is in us!

Moses lead the Israelites out of Egypt, out of bondage and slavery, to freedom and headed for the Promised Land.

They had lived as slaves for many years and knew what it was like to live in chains. When they left Egypt, they were free, physically, however because they had been slaves for so many years, they still lived as though they were in chains. Like the story about the elephants, they were conditioned to believe they were still slaves.

They had served Pharaoh, who had worked them hard, they had seen their peers mistreated and even killed. They didn't know what it was like to live in their newfound freedom.

There were many gods in that time and culture, therefore the Egyptians didn't know the one true God, The King of kings and Lord of lords. They didn't know God's character. They didn't know He is faithful to His promises, that He does not lie or that unlike the gods they were used to hearing about and know, that God was living and going to lead them into their promise land.

Imagine walking free, after many years enslaved. They wouldn't have known any other way of living.

'So, Christ has truly set us free. Now make sure that you stay free, and don't get tied up again in slavery to the law.' (Galatians 5.1 NLT)

Jesus not only died for our salvation but so we can live in freedom, truly liberated, in every area of our life. No longer wearing chains or living like slaves but living in the fullness of His perfect freedom.

God gave the promised land to Abraham, He used Moses to free the Israelites from slavery and bring them to its border. But the Israelites' lack of faith made that promise ineffective for them.

The Israelites complained constantly, which angered The Lord. It took forty years to do an eleven-day journey. Complaining and whingeing is not language and behaviour that we need to display as children of God. It is interesting all through these scriptures, that it angered God. Sometimes, on our way out of breakthrough into new seasons, we can be focused on what we don't have, on what we are lacking and not focusing on what God has delivered us from and His promises that

He has already fulfilled. It doesn't take long to look around us and see God's goodness displayed.

The Lord said to Moses to send out some men to explore the land of Canaan. (Numbers 13.1) Moses sent out spies to bring back a report of what was ahead, as the Lord had instructed. They saw a land of milk and honey. They also saw giants in the land.

The report the majority of the spies brought back to Moses, was all around fear, because of the giants that they saw. Then Caleb spoke up and quietened the drama going on and spoke of the fruit of the land, the goodness they saw, the milk and honey that was flowing. Caleb was expectant and wanting to possess this land.

Does this not sound like life in the world in which we live? Sometimes drama is loud, negativity is noisy, and we can lean into this, as it can be what is popular and even draw people in together.

I want to encourage us to be like Caleb. To see beyond the giants, to stop the noise and drama and to claim what God has promised you!

> We will not fully possess our blessing if we focus on the giants.

'Wherever you set foot, that land will be yours!' (Deuteronomy 11.24 NLT)
'Wherever you set foot, you will be on land I have given you.' (Joshua 1.3 NLT)

Giants are there to distract and to obstruct our view from what lies beyond all that God has for us. As we fix our eyes on the One in whom our help comes from, then we can slay the giant and enter the promised land and all that God has for us.

When I was twenty, I went to find out who I was and wanted to discover life for myself.

When I 'found myself', which of course was in Him, I had a relationship with God that I'd never experienced before. We can have a personal, intimate relationship with the Most High God for ourselves. In the Old Testament only the Priest could go into the Holy of Holies, but now we have permission, access and full authority to enter and live from that place. Selah!

Let's choose to be like Moses, Joshua and Caleb. People that see beyond the giants, people who are obedient and walk through, in spite of the noise and negativity around them. Let's choose not to whinge and whine and complain. Let's be people who trust in the One who not only see the Promised Land but possess it.

I want to possess every single promise that Christ has for me to possess!

> God can give us promises, but we need to conquer and claim them!

Let us always be on an adventure of discovering the mysteries of God, studying the word, and walking in all that God has for us.

God uses everything in our lives, He is faithful like no other. I do have to wonder if the Israelite's complaining and bickering, doubt and unbelief had anything to do with the delay.

Your past has got you to where you are today. Where you stand right now, at this time and place, is due to choices you've made.

Where you go from here, is up to you.

Are you going to allow the past to hold you back from entering all that is yours to possess? That is a big question which can ultimately determine the rest of your life.

We know in Jeremiah 29.11 (NLT) it says, *'For I know the plans I have for you', says the Lord. They are plans for good and not for disaster, to give you a future and a hope.'* Do you believe that? Do you want that?

What is holding you back from entering the Promised Land? Again, a big question.

God promises us every spiritual blessing. We can seek them our entire lives but not lay hold of them all.

'All praise to God, the Father of our Lord Jesus Christ, who has blessed us with every spiritual blessing in the heavenly realms because we are united with Christ.' (Ephesians 1.3 NLT)

God had given them the Promised Land when He made a covenant with Abraham. (Genesis 15) It was already theirs, they just needed to possess it.

We haven't even begun to tap into all that God has for us. To walk in the fullness of who we are and of what He wants us to experience and the fullness of life He has for us.

REST

In the last decade, I have been on a journey of discovering what true rest really is.

As I previously mentioned, when I did my chaplaincy training, I learnt about self-care, which was wonderful. I have put self-care practices into my life, and trained people I lead in doing the same. It is of the utmost importance. As crucial as this is, there is so much more to rest that I am learning.

A few years ago, through a study we were doing at church, we learnt about taking a sabbath day, to set aside to rest. I started to be intentional around setting aside, my Saturday as my sabbath.

God, after He made the Heavens and Earth, and every other thing, He rested on the seventh day. (Genesis 2.2,3) I think if God created a seventh day and chose to rest on that day, it was something He was intentional about. If God needs to demonstrate rest, what greater reason do we need to practice this?

I am intentional around what I do on my sabbath. I set aside time to be in God's presence, to read the word, to participate in a soak session, to be in nature or have a coffee at my favourite beach.

Early on in the sabbath journey, I remember thinking I don't feel any more refreshed than I use to, before being intentional around having a sabbath. Holy Spirit spoke to my heart and said, 'I want you to learn to rest your soul.' I then went on a journey of discovering what resting your soul means.

I love Psalm 23, particularly in The Passion Translation.

'The Lord is my best friend and my shepherd. I always have more than enough. He offers a resting place for me in His luxurious love. His tracks take me to an oasis of peace, the quiet brook of bliss. That's where He restores and revives my life. He opens before me pathways to God's pleasure and leads me along in His footsteps of righteousness so that I can bring honour to His name. Lord, even when Your path takes me through the valley of deepest darkness fear will never conquer me, for You already have! You remain close to me and lead me through it all the way. Your authority is my strength and my peace. The comfort of Your love takes away my fear. I'll never be lonely, for You are near. You become my delicious feast even when my enemies dare to fight. You anoint me with the fragrance of Your Holy Spirit; You give me all I can drink of You until my heart overflows. So why would I fear

the future? For Your goodness and love pursue me all the days of my life. Then afterward, when my life is through, I'll return to Your glorious presence to be forever with You!' (Psalm 23.1-6 TPT)

What a beautiful scripture to soak in.

Rest is a place that you and I can live from, not just on our day off or sabbath, but every day of our lives. When you discover that, there is no greater place to live.

I discovered that resting my soul meant that whilst still being true to who I am (how God wired me – being high thinker) I could, with the help of the Holy Spirit, stop for a moment trying to think about everything I had to, in my list-type brain. Then breath, relax and trust the One who holds my moment and my future in His perfect hands. I'm sure you've heard the saying 'let go and let God.' That has been a journey of outworking and when I walk in that, it's all kinds of amazing.

In writing this I do not pretend that this is an easy process, or that I even have it down pat. I have learnt the importance of laying down my mind, will and emotions, in return for His will. Not my will but Yours Lord, like our greatest example Jesus said to His Father.

Hebrews 4 (NLT) speaks about the rest of God. It is titled 'Promised Rest for God's People.' It says, *'Gods promise of entering His rest still stands, so we ought to tremble with fear that some of you might fail to experience it. For this good news – that God has prepared this rest – has been announced to us just as it was to them. But it did them no good because they didn't share the faith for those who listened to God. For only we who believe can enter His rest.'* (Hebrews 4.1-3 NLT)

The keys I get from this scripture is it's been prepared for us. How do we enter the promised rest of God? By believing, having faith and it goes on later in the chapter (verses 10, 11) to rest from your labours and by obedience.

I love that doing life with God is a partnership. I don't have to walk through life on my own, or in my own strength. I have Him right beside me, helping me with decisions and leaning on Him. My life is dependent on Him. As independent as I am, I have learnt to remain dependent on Him. Now again, with my temperament, I listen to the sweet, voice of Holy Spirit nudging me when I go into doing things and relying on myself in things. I am so grateful, beyond words on a page, that I have Him to lean on and rely on and depend on and rest in.

> When I let go and let God, I relinquish my rights, my will and lordship over my life and give God full access and right to be Lord over my life.

This has been key to living from a place of rest, for me.

I love the scripture in Matthew 11.28-30 (MSG), *'Are you tired? Worn out? Burned out on religion? Come to Me. Get away with Me and you'll recover your life. I'll show you how to take a real rest. Walk with Me and work with Me – watch how I do it.'* I love this next part. *'Learn the unforced rhythms of grace. I won't lay anything heavy or ill-fitting on you. Keep company with Me and you'll learn to live freely and lightly.'*

These words are spoken from the mouth of Jesus.

Have you ever felt heavy burdened or weighed down? I love that God knew us well enough to know we were never designed to carry burdens. That we can walk with Him, work with Him and recover our life. Jesus says that He will show us how to take real rest.

Jesus lived His life on Earth, from a place of rest.
He knew who He was, His purpose, His mission in life. He lived from a place of tranquillity, no matter the anarchy going on around Him.

Mark chapter four recounts the story of the disciples, who were in a boat and a fierce storm came up. Jesus was asleep. Jesus' friends were frantic, thinking that Jesus didn't care, because He didn't wake up panicked. Instead He remained calm, and using His authority, spoke to the storm, and it calmed down.

Did His friends even know who they were on the boat with? They were on there with the Saviour. I don't think they realised the magnitude of that, until well after He had died and rose again.

We have the honour and privilege of doing life, twenty-four seven with Jesus. We are in Him. Jesus wasn't brought into the drama and noise that was going on around Him. He was full of peace. (well, He is the Prince of Peace)

I don't want to be distracted by the noise going on around me, but to remain calm, full of peace and speak with authority, in who I am (and who's in me) to the storms that come and go.

If rest is something God is so passionate about, it's interesting we are living in a time where everyone's lives seem to be so busy. It's almost popular or even successful to say, 'I'm so busy.'

John 10.10, as we've read through the pages of this book, the enemy comes to steal, kill and destroy but Jesus has come that we may have life, and life abundant. I have to wonder if that applies to rest, in this context. Busyness would be what the enemy tries to bring to our life, to steal our rest and peace. Life abundant is living a life of intentional rest, practising rest and living from a place of rest, in our everyday lives.

Rest is a gift, that God has given us. We don't need to strive for it. We need to receive the gift that He gave us. *'Peace I leave with you; My peace I give you. I do not give to you as the world gives. Do not let your hearts be troubled and do not be afraid.'* (John 14.27 NIV)

I love that we are IN Him and He is IN us. In knowing this and living from this revelation we should be able to live from a place of rest.

'He raised us up with Christ the exalted One, and we ascended with Him into the glorious perfection and authority of the heavenly realm, for we are now co-seated as one with Christ!' (Ephesians 2.6 TPT)

If we are seated with Him in the heavenly realm, co-seated with Christ, (pause and think about that for a moment) we would be living from a place of rest.

'Let the peace of Christ [the inner calm of one who walks daily with Him] be the controlling factor in your hearts [deciding and settling questions that arise]. To this peace indeed you were called as members in one body [of believers]. And be thankful [to God always].' (Colossians 3.15 AMP)

I want to encourage you today, if you don't already, to be intentional about practising rest. To consider taking a sabbath. To not get so busy with the noise and goings on in the current culture, but to embark on the journey of living from a place of rest.

APP

- What chains are keeping you bound?
- What do you need to relinquish your rights to and give God lordship over in your life?
- What practises can you incorporate into your life to live from a place of rest?

CHAPTER 10
GO

'It's not about how much you do, but how much love you put into what you do that counts.'
(Mother Theresa)

Well, we have got to the last and final chapter of this book.

Lots of subjects, have been covered and I hope through the pages of this book you have embarked on a journey of finding out who you are, why you are here and understanding and accepting the way God has designed and created you.

The journey of discovering this, is life changing and freeing, beyond words.

Now I'm going to say something that is going to sound contrary to what I've said in the first nine chapters. Hear my heart on this. Life is not all about you!

I love that you now, are on the journey and having adventures of discovering who you are and walking in the fullness of who you are in Christ. While that is amazing and part of the purpose and heart behind this book, there is another reason.

When we know who we are and walking in the fullness of Christ and in freedom, hopefully similar revelations are being unlocked in others around you.

Jesus left Heaven, came to the Earth in the most vulnerable form, as a baby. Jesus grew up knowing who He was, His mission, and fulfilled His purpose so that we could live in the finished work of Christ.

We know from Jesus' time on the Earth that He served others and taught us, by being the greatest example of extravagant love ever given to humanity.

THE GREATEST COMMANDMENT

Jesus' life was about two core messages: loving God and loving people. Sounds easy, hey! Anyone who has breathed more than five minutes knows loving people can be harder than it sounds.

Jesus talks about it in Mark 12.30,31. I love how it says it in The Passion and New Living Translations.

Jesus answered him, 'The most important of all the commandments is this: 'The Lord Yahweh, our God, is one!' You are to love the Lord Yahweh, your God, with every passion of your heart, with all the energy of your being, with every thought that is within you, and with all your strength. This is the great and supreme commandment. And the second is this: 'You must love your neighbour in the same way you love yourself.' You will never find a greater commandment than these yourself. You will never find a greater commandment than these. (TPT)

'And you must love the Lord your God with all your heart, all your soul, all your mind, and all your strength.' The second is equally important: 'Love your neighbour as yourself.' No other commandment is greater than these.' (NLT)

> It is our mission to
> 1. Love God and 2. Love people.

Under the old covenant there were 613 commandments. In the new covenant, Jesus gave us two commandments to live by. The purpose of the previous chapters on understanding yourself, is so you can love and understand others around you, even people unlike you.

Until we have a healthy godly love for ourselves, how can we love our neighbour as we love ourselves?

WHO IS YOUR NEIGHBOUR?

Your neighbour is anyone in your world. This includes your significant others, your family, your friends, your coffee barista, your work colleagues or anyone you come in contact with.

Casting Crowns is a band I love. A lot of the lyrics of their songs are challenging and speak the truth in love.

Their song 'If we are the body' describes it so beautifully. Take time to look it up and let the words, challenge and encourage you. In the chorus it challenges us that if we are the body of Christ why isn't Jesus being demonstrated to those in our congregations and to the wider community?

As I've mentioned, you and I are the church and I take the words in this song as a personal mandate. Am I being the church? Am I displaying Jesus to the people in my world? Am I loving people, speaking truth and hope for their futures?

There is a line in the bridge of this song that made me sit back in my seat. It has been a reminder to me when I've wanted to keep walking, to get my task done and not take time for the one. *Jesus paid much too high a price, for us to pick and choose who should come.'* The first time I heard these words, it was like a wave of conviction came over me.

Jesus paid a price for us, yes, you and me. He also died for every person. Every person includes the people I find annoying, the person that may be far from God, the broken or the angry person and even those that do heinous things. Jesus died for all of humanity.

My natural bent is not to be an evangelist. My Dad on the other hand, wow, he turns around and people get saved. We will be sitting in a café having a coffee and we see the waiter with a bandage on their hand and he'll ask to pray for them. He has seen many healings and witnessed to hundreds of people, one on one, and shared the testimony of how God saved his life.

There have been times my Mum and I have been embarrassed and thought 'Oh Garry', or 'Dad' and it doesn't take us long to get over that and think 'boy, imagine what the world would be like without people like my Dad.' There would be many people who would never hear the gospel if my Dad didn't speak to people this way.

Now I'm not saying I have to go and preach on the street corners or be like my Dad in that area. I am saying it is good for us to be aware that every person Jesus died for, has been redeemed and made a righteous son of God, some just haven't had the revelation of that yet.

We see people in front of us and can be tempted to make judgments on what we see. We don't know their story, their life traumas, even what their morning has been like, so how dare we make judgements and treat people unkindly.

Jesus loved people. His twelve that He 'did life' with, were not perfect people. Jesus, knowing all, would have known that one of them was going to betray Him and another one was going to deny Him, not once, but three times.

You know, every one of those twelve, had a piece of Jesus' destiny. Yes, even Judas.

There has always been this justice pocket in me that has disliked the attitude of people thinking they are better than anyone else. Jesus died for every person, rich, poor, the ones that look the part and the ones that don't present quite as well. A person who is broken and struggles in life, deserves dignity and kindness and to be given hope that they too can walk in freedom and eternal life.

The last few years I have been intentional with being present in the moments. I tend to get task-focused if I am at work, or even need to go to the supermarket to pick something up. In the mornings I pray 'Lord, not my will, but Yours be done in my life today.' Now instead of just ticking off my list for the day, I look for opportunities when I'm picking up my coffee, or going to the supermarket, or in a rush or wanting to be introverted, to smile or just stop and be present for the person standing in front of me.

Life is not all about me! There's something bigger at play.

Now, I'm not going to touch on eschatology, as there are many different views. What I am going to say is if you knew your friend had won the lottery, you saw their name had been called and they had the winning ticket but didn't say anything, what a shame that they could have missed their chance of a lifetime to have what was theirs, they just didn't know it yet.

Likewise, eternal life, freedom, abundant life is theirs, here and now, some people just aren't aware of that, yet.

'Those who are loved by God, let His love continually pour from you to one another, because God is love. Everyone who loves is fathered by God and experiences an intimate knowledge of Him. The one who doesn't love has yet to know God, for God is love. The light of God's love shined within us when He sent His matchless Son into the world so that we might live through Him. This is love: He loved us long before we loved Him. It was His love, not ours. He proved it by sending His son to be the pleasing sacrificial offering to take away our sins. Delightfully loved ones, if He loved us with such tremendous love, then "loving one another" should be

our way of life! No one has ever gazed upon the fullness of God's splendour. But if we love one another, God makes His permanent home in us, and we make our permanent home in Him, and His love is brought to its full expression in us. And He has given us His Spirit within us so that we can have the assurance that He lives in us and that we live in Him. Moreover, we have seen with our own eyes and can testify to the truth that Father God has sent His Son to be the Saviour of the world. Those who give thanks that Jesus is the Son of God live in God and God lives in them. We have come into an intimate experience with God's love, and we trust in the love He has for us. God is love! Those who are living in love are living in God, and God lives through them. By living in God, love has been brought to its full expression in us so that we may fearlessly face the day of judgment, because all that Jesus now is, so are we in this world. Love never brings fear, for fear is always related to punishment. But love's perfection drives the fear of punishment far from our hearts. Whoever walks constantly afraid of punishment has not reached 'love's perfection. Our love for others is our grateful response to the love God first demonstrated to us. Anyone can say, "I love God," yet have hatred toward another believer. This makes him a phony, because if you don't love a brother or sister, whom you can see, how can you truly love God, whom you can't see? For He has given us this command: whoever loves God must also demonstrate love to others.'
(1 John 4.7-21 TPT)

We could sit and mull over this scripture for hours. There is so much we can apply to our lives.

We have been given love, extravagant love, so why would we want to keep that to ourselves? It is a sign we are Christ followers, that we love one another.

'One another' embraces everyone.

Embracing everyone, not just the lovely people in our world, or the people who agree and are like us, but every person. Keep those words of that song in our heads *Jesus paid much too high a price for us to pick and choose who should come.'*

One of my favourite scriptures is Isaiah 61. Many years ago, I received a prophetic word over my life and the prophet said this is my mandate, which I had already felt. You don't need a prophet to come and say that this is your mandate today. Would you read these words and take hold of this for yourself?

Isaiah 61 (NLT) says, *'The Spirit of the Sovereign Lord is upon me, for the Lord has anointed me to bring good news to the poor. He has sent me to comfort the broken-hearted and to proclaim that captives will be released, and prisoners will be freed. He has sent me to tell those who mourn that the time of the Lord's favour has come, and with it, the day of God's anger against their enemies. To all who mourn in Israel, He will give a crown of beauty for ashes, a joyous blessing instead of mourning, festive praise instead of despair. In their righteousness, they will be like great oaks that the Lord has planted for His own glory. They will rebuild the ancient ruins, repairing cities destroyed long ago. They will revive them, though they have been deserted for many generations. Foreigners will be your servants. They will feed your flocks and plow your fields and tend your vineyards. You will be called priests of the Lord, ministers of our God. You will feed on the treasures of the nations and boast in their riches. Instead of shame and dishonour, you will enjoy a double share of honour. You will possess a double portion of prosperity in your land, and everlasting joy will be yours. 'For I, the Lord, love justice. I hate robbery and wrongdoing. I will faithfully reward my people for their suffering and make an everlasting covenant with them. Their descendants will be recognised and honoured among the nations. Everyone will realise that they are a people the Lord has blessed. I am overwhelmed with joy in the Lord my God! For He has dressed me with the clothing of salvation and draped me in a robe of righteousness. I am like a bridegroom dressed for his wedding or a bride with her jewels. The Sovereign Lord will show His justice to the nations of the world. Everyone will praise Him! His righteousness will be like a garden in early spring, with plants springing up everywhere.'*

Do you not think this is a time for everyone in the world, in which we live to hear the good news? It is time to encounter the God that loves them, beyond measure, and died for them to walk in joy, liberty and salvation. A time in which generations need to receive a crown of beauty for their ashes.

In the first few verses of this chapter, it says who is called to do this. It doesn't leave this to the evangelists. It says me. The Spirit of the Sovereign Lord is upon me, for the Lord has anointed me to bring good news to the poor. He has sent me to comfort the broken hearted and to proclaim that captives will be released, and prisoners will be freed. He has sent me to tell those who mourn that the time of the Lord's favour has come.

How many people do you see that need comfort for their broken heart or joy for mourning, especially in the time and season we find ourselves in? In some people's lives, we may be the only Jesus they ever meet. Let's not miss an opportunity.

As I said you don't have to be anyone you are not, however we know about the great commission Jesus gave to His disciples. No matter what our temperament, five-fold ministry gift or any other gift, the great commission includes you and me.

Our lives should display the glory of God. We don't need to be weird about it. We are called to carry His presence, His abundant life, His joy, hope and peace, so that people can't help but want what we have.

We are living in a day and age where people need hope. At church we say 'hope has a name and His name is Jesus.' You and I display Jesus. We are hope carriers!

> When we know our worth and who we are in Christ, it carries power to unlock and release other people to see their worth and value.

In John 1.42 it says, *'Then Andrew brought Simon to meet Jesus. Looking intently at Simon, Jesus said, 'Your name is Simon, son of John – but you will be called Cephas.' (which means 'Peter'* NLT)

Jesus always saw more than the person standing in front of Him. Jesus saw their potential. Jesus called out the man who Peter was.

As I've previously stated, we too can ask to see people with Jesus's lens. To look beyond their behaviour, the walls and what is going on in front of us, and call out the person's destiny and their identity, which is firstly a child of God.

'But the Holy Spirit produces this kind of fruit in our lives: love, joy, peace, patience, kindness, goodness, faithfulness, gentleness and self-control.' (Galatians 5.22, 23 NLT)

Love is a fruit of the spirit. We have the Holy Spirit that produces this fruit in our lives.

I have made jokes that my patience fruit is like a dried-up sultana as it is not my flourishing, plumpest fruit. Truth is that as I abide in Christ, and remember I am in Christ and He is in me, therefore I have access to the patience Jesus is. Selah!

'So, chosen by God for this new life of love, dress in the wardrobe God picked out for you: compassion, kindness, humility, quiet strength, discipline. Be even-tempered, content with second place, quick to forgive an offense. Forgive as quickly and completely as the Master forgave you. And regardless of what else you put on,

wear love. It's your basic, all-purpose garment. Never be without it.' (Colossians 3.12-14 MSG)

'Above all, clothe yourselves with love, which binds us all together in perfect harmony.' (Colossians 3.14 NLT)

We can wake up every day, and as part of our declarations we can clothe ourselves in love. A love that binds us all together in perfect harmony. If we all did this, daily, would this not transform the world in which we live?

It is easier to love others knowing who we are, and that we are loved.

> Walking in love and being kind is more important than being right.

I want to end this chapter and this book with giving glory to God. The reason we are all on the Earth, is to bring all glory to Him.

This book has been a long, long, long, time coming. I would not be the woman I am today if it was not for my precious Lord and Saviour. I cannot even begin to express the love I have for Him.

God wants you to live your best life here and now, to be transformed into His likeness, as you have been created in His beautiful image. He wants you to know and live in Him, and realise you have every gift you need to live an abundant life. He wants you to align yourself with Kingdom economy and language and walk, head held high, releasing His power in your life and unlocking identity and power in other people, all for His glory.

I pray that you will go back and do the exercises and practical applications throughout these chapters.

I pray this will be more than words on a page, or another book you have on your bookshelf. I pray the words are alive and open the eyes of your understanding and unlock all that you are in Him, today, that your life is never the same again.

Know that you are loved, and you are blessed!
Much love Kylie xo

APP

- How can you practically love your neighbour?
- What can you do as an act of kindness for someone in your world?
- Like Jesus renamed Peter, spend some time with Holy Spirit and let Him reveal who you are, maybe your new name?

www.ingramcontent.com/pod-product-compliance
Lightning Source LLC
Chambersburg PA
CBHW072335300426
44109CB00042B/1610